I0616673

SYSTEMATIC THEOLOGY FOR TEENS IN 90 DAYS

UNDERSTAND WHAT YOU BELIEVE, WHY IT
MATTERS, AND WHAT THE BIBLE TEACHES
ABOUT GOD, JESUS, AND THE CHRISTIAN FAITH

RADIANT FAITH

INTRODUCTION

Cole had always been the kid with all the answers in youth group. He could recite Bible verses from memory, had perfect attendance at Sunday school since kindergarten, and even led worship on occasion. His faith felt rock-solid, unshakeable, built on years of Christian education and a supportive church community. He was ready to take on the world.

Then came his first philosophy class at State University.

"If God is all-good and all-powerful, why does evil exist?" Professor Martinez posed the question with a slight smile, as if he'd asked it a thousand times before. Cole raised his hand confidently, ready to give the standard answer about free will that had always satisfied his youth pastor. But as the professor's follow-up questions came like rapid fire, Cole found himself struggling: "But what about natural disasters? What about children born with terminal illnesses? If God knew this would happen, why create at all?"

For the first time in his life, Cole sat in stunned silence.

The simple answers that had carried him through eighteen years of faith suddenly felt inadequate, even hollow. Doubt crept in like water through cracks in a foundation he'd thought was solid concrete. Was his faith built on sand after all?

That night, Cole called his youth pastor in a panic.

"I think I'm losing my faith," he whispered into the phone.

His pastor did not rush to reassure him or shut the conversation down. Instead, he said something that caught Cole off guard.

"No, Cole. I think you're finally finding it. Real faith is not about having all the answers. It is about learning how to ask the right questions."

That conversation stayed with Cole. It changed the way he understood what was happening inside him. Instead of walking away from his beliefs when they felt shaky, he leaned in. He began to read more carefully, think more honestly, and wrestle with the questions he had been afraid to voice.

Along the way, he discovered that he was not alone. Some of the greatest thinkers in Christian history had asked the very same questions that were bothering him. Their faith had not collapsed because of those questions. It had grown deeper because of them.

Cole slowly realized that doubt was not the enemy of faith. Shallow thinking was.

Over the next four years, his faith became stronger. Not because it was never challenged, but because it had been tested. What emerged was something he now describes as an unshakeable faith, rooted not in avoiding questions, but in facing them honestly and walking through them with God.

Building Faith That Lasts

This book exists for one crucial reason: to prevent you from experiencing the faith crisis that blindsides so many young Christians when they encounter the real world. But more than that, it's designed to help you build something better than crisis-proof faith—it's designed to help you build antifragile faith that actually grows stronger under pressure.

Too many Christian teenagers graduate from high school with what we might call "greenhouse faith"—beliefs that thrive in the controlled environment of Christian family and church but wither when exposed to the harsh winds of secular university, workplace skepticism, or personal tragedy.

This book is about transplanting your faith from the greenhouse to the real world.

Our goal isn't to give you a list of pat answers to memorize. Instead, we're going to equip you with a robust theological framework—a systematic way of thinking about God, humanity, and reality that transforms abstract doctrines into living principles. These principles will guide your decision-making when you're facing peer pressure, inform your relationships when you're navigating dating and friendship, and shape your worldview when professors or colleagues challenge your beliefs.

Systematic theology might sound intimidating, but it's simply the practice of understanding what the Bible teaches about the big questions of life and how those teachings fit together into a coherent whole. It's the difference between knowing isolated Bible verses and understanding the grand story of which those verses are a part.

It's the difference between having Sunday school answers and possessing mature, thoughtful convictions.

Who This Book Is For

If you've picked up this book, chances are you're tired of being treated like your faith should be simple. You're ready to move beyond "Jesus loves you" and "just have faith" to engage with the deeper questions that keep you awake at night. You want to understand not just what you believe, but why you believe it—and how those beliefs should shape every aspect of your life.

This book is specifically written for Christian teenagers who find themselves in one of these situations:

- The Questioner: You love God, but you also love thinking. You're not satisfied with surface-level answers, and you sometimes worry that asking hard questions makes you a bad Christian.
- The Challenger: You're heading to college or already finding yourself in environments where your faith is questioned or even attacked. You need more than childhood Sunday school lessons to navigate these conversations.
- The Seeker: You've grown up in the church, but you're starting to wonder if your faith is really your own or just something you inherited.
- The Leader: You're already influencing others through worship, teaching, or friendship. You recognize that influence comes with responsibility, and you want to be equipped to guide others well.
- The Doubter: You've hit some bumps in your faith journey. Instead of running from your doubts, you want to work through them honestly and emerge stronger.

You want to develop the confidence to discuss and defend your beliefs with peers and adults without sounding like you're parroting someone else's words. You desire to build an unshakeable faith foundation that can withstand real-world challenges and doubts, understanding complex theological concepts in ways that connect to your daily life.

Why This Book Is Different

Walk into any Christian bookstore and you'll find dozens of books promising to strengthen teenage faith. So what makes this one different? Three key distinctions set this book apart:

Principle-Based Learning Over Answer Memorization: Most apologetics resources for teenagers focus on memorizing responses to common objections. While knowing these responses can be helpful, this approach often fails when you encounter variations of these questions or entirely new challenges. Instead, this book teaches you the underlying principles of systematic theology that will help you think through any challenge you encounter.

We also recognize that your generation learns differently than previous ones. You don't need more facts; you need frameworks for processing and evaluating information. You don't just need to know what Christians believe; you need to understand why Christian beliefs are compelling compared to alternatives. Rather than giving you a fish, we're teaching you to fish.

Real-World Application Over Academic Theory: This book bridges the gap between theological concepts and daily life by showing you how these principles apply to situations you actually face: navigating social media, choosing a college major, handling conflict with parents, dating relationships, career decisions, and social justice issues.

Progressive Complexity Over Information Dumping: This book meets you where you are and takes you on a carefully planned journey from simple concepts to complex understanding. Each chapter builds on the previous one, creating a systematic framework that grows in sophistication without losing accessibility.

Your Journey Through Foundational Truth

Over the next twelve chapters, you'll embark on a carefully structured journey through the foundational principles of systematic theology. Think of it as building a house—we'll start with the foundation and work our way up, ensuring each level is solid before we move to the next.

The Foundation: Who God Is (Chapters 1-3)

We begin with the doctrine of God because everything else depends on getting this right. You'll explore what it means that God is Trinity, how divine attributes shape our understanding of reality, and why the character of God matters for daily decision-making.

The Framework: How God Relates to Creation (Chapters 4-6)

Next, we'll examine how God interacts with the world He made. You'll dive into questions about divine sovereignty and human responsibility, the problem of evil and suffering, and how prayer and providence work together.

The Story: God's Plan for Humanity (Chapters 7-9)

Here we'll explore the grand narrative of Scripture: creation, fall, redemption, and restoration. You'll discover how understanding this overarching story helps you make sense of everything from current events to personal struggles.

The Application: Living Out Biblical Truth (Chapters 10-12)

The final section focuses on practical theology—how biblical truth shapes the way we live. You'll explore Christian ethics, the nature and mission of the church, and what the Bible teaches about the future.

Each chapter follows a consistent structure designed to maximize your learning:

- Opening scenarios that illustrate why the theological principle matters
- Biblical foundation examining what Scripture teaches
- Historical perspective on how Christians have understood these truths
- Modern applications specific to contemporary teenage life
- Honest engagement with common objections and criticisms
- Practical exercises for applying what you've learned

Throughout the journey, you'll encounter case studies of teenagers wrestling with real-world applications of these principles. You'll meet Eden as she navigates questions about evolution and creation in her biology class, and Joseph as he works through the tension between God's sovereignty and human responsibility after his grandfather's death.

These stories aren't theoretical—they're based on real situations that Christian teenagers face every day.

Embracing the Journey

Here's what I want you to understand before you turn the page: the journey you're about to begin will change you. You can't engage seriously with the deep truths of Christian theology and remain the same person. Your faith will be challenged, your assumptions will be questioned, and your understanding will be stretched.

This isn't a comfortable process—growth never is.

But here's what I promise you: if you're willing to wrestle with the big questions, if you're committed to moving from simple faith to mature understanding, you'll emerge from this journey with something invaluable. You'll have confidence that comes not from ignorance of challenges to your faith, but from having worked through those challenges thoughtfully. You'll have convictions that are truly your own, forged in the fire of honest inquiry and biblical study.

You'll have the tools to engage with the deepest questions of existence —not just as someone who has been told what to think, but as someone who has learned how to think.

This book is an invitation to join the ranks of thinking Christians throughout history who have refused to settle for shallow faith. It's a call to develop the kind of robust theological understanding that can engage with university professors, workplace skeptics, and personal tragedies without crumbling. It's a challenge to become the kind of Christian who makes the faith more attractive to others because of the depth and thoughtfulness of your convictions.

The world doesn't need more Christians who can't explain what they believe or why they believe it.

The world needs Christians who have wrestled with the hard questions and emerged with unshakeable confidence in the truth and beauty of the gospel. The world needs Christians who can engage with complex ideas, navigate difficult conversations, and provide compelling reasons for the hope that they have.

The question is: are you ready to become that kind of Christian?

If your answer is yes, then turn the page. Your journey into the depths of systematic theology—and the transformation of your faith from simple to mature—begins now.

Introduction Toolbox: Words for the Journey

- **Systematic Theology**: This is the practice of looking at the big questions of life and seeing how the answers in the Bible fit together into one coherent story.
- **Antifragile Faith**: This describes a faith that is built to last because it actually gets stronger when it is tested by the real world rather than crumbling under pressure.
- **Greenhouse Faith**: This is a type of belief that does well in the safe and controlled environment of a church or a Christian home but struggles when it faces the harsh winds of university or workplace skepticism.
- **Robust Framework**: This is a solid way of thinking about God and humanity that helps you turn abstract ideas into living principles you can actually use to make daily decisions.

1

THE GOD WHO HIDES IN PLAIN SIGHT

The Great Divine Divide

Yⁿou walk into a coffee shop with your best friend, and you both order the same drink from the same barista who's having the same rough morning. Yet somehow, one of you leaves feeling grateful for human connection while the other just got their caffeine fix. The same experience, completely different takeaways.

This happens with God too.

The same evidence that convinces one person of God's existence can leave another person completely unmoved. A breathtaking sunrise might fill someone with worship while their friend sees atmospheric particles scattering light wavelengths. A narrow escape from danger could feel like divine protection to one person and lucky timing to another.

Here's what's wild about this divide: it's not primarily about intelligence or education.

Think about it. Some of history's brightest minds have been devoted believers, while others have been convinced atheists. Nobel Prize winners line up on both sides of the God question. College professors teach in the same hallways and reach opposite conclusions about ultimate reality.

So what's really going on here?

The answer lies in something philosophers call our "interpretive framework." This is basically the lens through which we see the world, and it's shaped by three major factors that work together like ingredients in a recipe.

Our Starting Assumptions Shape What We See as Evidence

Before we even begin looking for God, we already have beliefs about what kinds of things are possible. If you start with the assumption that only physical, measurable things are real, then spiritual experiences will automatically get filtered out or explained away. But if you begin with openness to spiritual reality, the same experiences become potential evidence.

These starting points aren't usually chosen consciously. They develop over time through education, relationships, and life experiences.

Personal Experiences Create Filters

Your personal history acts like a filter that either opens or closes you to spiritual reality. Someone who grew up experiencing what they believed were answered prayers might be more open to seeing God's hand in everyday events. Meanwhile, someone who prayed desperately for something that never came might develop skepticism about divine involvement in human affairs.

Neither response is necessarily wrong. Both are human reactions to real experiences.

Cultural and Family Background Influence Everything

The family and culture you grew up in provide the initial framework for interpreting spiritual experiences. Some families celebrate every good thing as a blessing and interpret challenges as opportunities for growth. Other families approach life more pragmatically, looking for natural explanations and practical solutions.

Consider Tessa and her roommate Jenny. Tessa grew up in a family where every sunset was seen as God's artwork and every answered prayer was celebrated. Her parents pointed out spiritual lessons in daily experiences and spoke openly about feeling God's presence during difficult times.

Jenny came from a household where natural phenomena were explained purely scientifically and coincidences were just that—coincidences. Her parents valued critical thinking and taught her to look for logical explanations rather than spiritual ones.

When they both witnessed the same miraculous recovery of a friend from serious illness, their interpretive frameworks led to completely different conclusions. Tessa saw God's healing hand at work, while Jenny saw the remarkable but explainable power of modern medicine and the human body's resilience.

Neither was being unreasonable.

Understanding this divide is crucial for two reasons. First, it builds confidence in your own faith by helping you realize that belief in God isn't about lacking intelligence or ignoring evidence. Second, it helps you engage respectfully with those who disagree, recognizing that they're often looking at the same world through a different lens rather than simply being stubborn or blind.

The question isn't whether God leaves evidence of his existence, but whether we have eyes to see it.

Head Knowledge vs Heart Connection

You probably know tons of facts about your favorite celebrity. Their birthday, hometown, career highlights, relationship history, and maybe even their coffee order. But if you bumped into them at a grocery store, would they recognize you? Would they know your name, your struggles, or what makes you laugh?

That's the difference between knowing about someone and actually knowing them.

The same principle applies to God, and understanding this distinction might be the most important thing you learn about faith.

Head Knowledge vs Heart Knowledge

Academic knowledge about theology, biblical history, and Christian doctrine is valuable and important. Learning about God's character, studying biblical languages, and understanding church history all matter. These things form the foundation of mature faith and help us avoid dangerous misunderstandings about who God is.

But head knowledge represents just one type of understanding.

Heart knowledge is different entirely. It's the kind of knowing that comes through relationship, experience, and personal encounter. When you know someone with your heart, you understand not just facts about them but how they think, what they care about, and how they respond in different situations.

This distinction helps explain something that puzzles many people: why some individuals with deep theological education can still feel spiritually empty, while others with simple faith experience profound connection with the divine.

It's not that education is bad or that ignorance is better. It's that information alone doesn't create relationship.

Personal Relationship Requires Communication

Think about your closest friendships. They weren't built by reading about each other or studying personality profiles. They developed through conversation, shared experiences, and mutual trust. You learned about your friends by spending time with them, talking through problems together, and being present during both good times and hard times.

Relationship with God works similarly.

Personal connection requires ongoing communication, not just information gathering. Prayer becomes conversation rather than reciting memorized words. Bible reading shifts from academic study to listening for God's voice. Worship transforms from performance to authentic expression of love and gratitude.

This doesn't minimize the importance of theological knowledge. Rather, it provides the context where that knowledge comes alive and becomes personally meaningful.

Experiential Knowledge Through Trust and Practice

Experiential knowledge comes through trust, obedience, and spiritual practices. When you actually try following Jesus's teachings about forgiveness, you discover whether they work in real life. When you practice generosity, you learn firsthand about God's provision. When you choose vulnerability in prayer, you experience whether God really cares about your struggles.

This kind of knowledge can't be downloaded or transferred through lectures. It must be lived.

On the outside, Charles looked like someone with a strong faith. He could recite Bible verses from memory and explain theological ideas that impressed his youth pastor. He knew the difference between justification and sanctification, between being made right with God and learning to live differently day by day. He could outline the major theological views and regularly won Bible trivia competitions.

But when his parents divorced, all of that knowledge suddenly felt useless.

The verses about God's love sounded hollow. The theological ideas he once understood so clearly did not touch the anger, sadness, and confusion he felt. Everything he knew about God seemed strangely disconnected from what he was actually going through.

What changed was not a new lesson or a deeper study.

It began when Charles started praying honestly. Instead of speaking about God in the third person, he began speaking directly to Him. He brought his fear, his frustration, and his disappointment into prayer without trying to clean them up or sound spiritual.

This was not impressive theology. It was not polished faith. It was real conversation.

Over time, his faith became steady and personal. His biblical knowledge did not disappear, but it finally had somewhere to land. The same verses that once felt distant began to speak to his life because he was reading them as words from someone he knew, not just information he had memorized.

Head knowledge and heart knowledge are not enemies. Strong faith needs both. But knowledge only comes alive when it grows out of relationship.

And relationship always comes first.

God's Fingerprints in Ordinary Moments

God doesn't only speak through burning bushes and dramatic miracles. His clearest communication often happens through the most ordinary things you encounter every single day.

Theologians call this "general revelation"—the ways God reveals himself to all people through the natural world, moral conscience, and human culture. Unlike special revelation (which we'll explore when we talk about the Bible), general revelation is available to everyone, everywhere, at all times.

This universal revelation explains something fascinating: why people from every culture throughout history have sensed the divine and developed moral systems, even when separated by oceans and centuries.

Creation Displays God's Character

The natural world functions like God's business card, displaying his power, creativity, and intricate design in ways accessible to everyone. You don't need theological training to feel awe when standing beneath a star-filled sky or to notice the incredible precision required for life to exist on Earth.

Consider the complexity of a single human cell. It contains more information than the entire Encyclopedia Britannica, with molecular machines that operate with precision beyond anything humans have engineered. The DNA in your body, if stretched out, would reach from Earth to the sun and back multiple times.

These aren't just cool science facts. They're glimpses into the mind of the Creator.

Even the basic mathematical principles that govern the universe suggest design rather than randomness. The fact that human minds can discover and understand these patterns points to something beyond mere chance. Why should random evolutionary processes produce brains capable of appreciating beauty or pondering infinity?

Universal Moral Awareness

Perhaps even more compelling is the moral conscience that appears in every human culture. Despite vast differences in customs and practices, certain moral intuitions show up everywhere: concepts of justice, care for the vulnerable, and recognition that some actions are simply wrong regardless of consequences.

This shared moral awareness can't be easily explained by evolutionary survival alone.

Why do people sacrifice their own interests for strangers? Why does injustice make us angry even when it doesn't affect us personally? Why do we feel guilty about actions no one else will ever discover?

These universal moral intuitions point beyond human invention to a moral standard that transcends cultural preferences and individual opinions. They suggest we're made in the image of a moral God who has written basic ethical principles into the fabric of human nature.

Cultural Expressions of Transcendence

Human cultures universally create art, music, literature, and rituals that reach beyond mere survival needs. Every society develops ways to express beauty, meaning, and connection to something greater than themselves.

This creative drive reflects our nature as image-bearers of the ultimate Creator.

Even secular artists and writers often describe their work as tapping into something beyond themselves—receiving inspiration rather than simply manufacturing products. The fact that humans universally hunger for meaning, beauty, and transcendence suggests we're designed for relationship with the divine.

Consider Maya who was struggling to connect with her agnostic lab partner during biology class while studying cellular structures. Instead of launching into theological arguments, she began pointing out the incredible precision and beauty they were observing under the microscope.

Her partner admitted feeling a sense of awe and wondering "where all this amazing complexity comes from."

This opened a natural conversation about design and purpose that felt curious rather than confrontational. Maya wasn't trying to prove God's existence through scientific evidence. She was simply helping her partner notice what was already there—the fingerprints of divine creativity visible in the microscopic world.

Recognizing God's Fingerprints

Learning to recognize general revelation helps you see God's finger-prints everywhere and provides common ground for conversations with people from different backgrounds. You can appreciate a sunset with an atheist friend, discuss the mystery of consciousness with an agnostic classmate, or explore questions of meaning with someone from another religious tradition.

These shared experiences of wonder, moral conviction, and creative inspiration create natural bridges for deeper conversations about ultimate reality.

The God who hides in plain sight leaves traces of himself in every ordinary moment, waiting to be discovered by anyone with eyes to see.

God's Unfolding Story Through Time

Imagine trying to explain quantum physics to a five-year-old. You wouldn't start with complex equations or abstract theories. Instead, you'd begin with simple concepts they could grasp, gradually building understanding over time as their minds developed and their knowledge expanded.

God took a similar approach with humanity.

Rather than downloading the complete revelation of his nature and plans all at once, divine revelation unfolded gradually throughout history, building from basic truths about God's existence and character to increasingly specific revelations about his purposes and promises.

This progressive revelation explains many questions that puzzle Bible readers and strengthens confidence in Scripture's reliability and coherence.

Foundational Truths Come First

Early revelations established foundational truths about God's character and basic requirements for human relationship with him. When God first spoke to Abraham, the message was relatively simple: leave your homeland, trust me, and I'll bless you and make you a great nation.

God didn't immediately explain the Trinity, outline salvation through grace, or detail end-times prophecy. He started with fundamental concepts Abraham could understand and act upon.

Similarly, the moral laws given to Moses addressed the immediate needs of a nomadic people learning to live as God's covenant community. These laws established basic principles about justice, worship, and social order that would serve as stepping stones toward fuller revelation.

The early revelations weren't incomplete or wrong. They were perfectly suited for their time and purpose, laying groundwork for what would come later.

Building Upon Previous Knowledge

Historical events and prophetic messages built upon previous revelations, adding layers of understanding without contradicting earlier truths. Each new revelation provided additional clarity while remaining consistent with what God had already revealed about his character.

The prophets didn't introduce completely new concepts about God. Instead, they applied foundational truths to specific situations, called people back to forgotten principles, and pointed toward future fulfillment of God's promises.

When Isaiah spoke about a coming Messiah, he built upon existing promises to David about an eternal kingdom. When Jeremiah prophesied about a new covenant, he referenced the existing covenant structure while pointing toward its transformation.

This progressive building created a unified story rather than a collection of disconnected religious ideas.

Jesus as the Ultimate Revelation

Jesus Christ represents the culmination and clarification of all previous revelation. He didn't replace what came before but fulfilled and explained it. In Jesus, abstract concepts about God's character became concrete and personal. Symbolic rituals found their ultimate meaning. Prophetic promises reached their intended destination.

This is why New Testament writers repeatedly used phrases like "as it was written" and "this fulfilled what was spoken." They weren't forcing connections where none existed but recognizing how Jesus brought clarity to revelations that had been building toward this moment throughout history.

Consider Marcus who was confused when his atheist friend pointed out apparent contradictions between Old Testament laws and New Testament teachings about grace. His friend argued that if the Bible was truly God's word, it shouldn't seem to contradict itself about fundamental issues.

By studying how God's revelation progressed—from basic moral laws needed by an ancient nomadic people to the full revelation of his character in Jesus—Marcus began to see the Bible as a unified story rather than a collection of conflicting rules.

He learned that ceremonial laws served temporary purposes while moral principles remained constant. He discovered that what looked like contradiction was actually progression, like comparing elementary math worksheets with advanced calculus problems.

This helped him explain to his friend why Christians don't follow every Old Testament regulation while still believing the entire Bible represents God's word. The regulations weren't wrong for their time, but they pointed toward something greater that was fully revealed in Christ.

Understanding progressive revelation transforms how we read Scripture, moving us from confusion about apparent contradictions to appreciation for God's masterful unfolding of truth across centuries of human history.

Chapter 1 Toolbox: Seeing the Divine

- **Worldview**: This is the invisible lens or the set of assumptions you use to see and make sense of everything in reality . It is shaped by your background and your experiences and the things you were taught as you grew up.
- **General Revelation**: These are the ways God reveals Himself to all people through the natural world and the human conscience and our shared culture. It is available to everyone

everywhere at all times and shows off the power and the creativity of the Creator.

- **Progressive Revelation**: This describes how God did not download all His truth at once but instead unfolded His plan and His character gradually throughout history . He started with basic concepts and built on them over time as human understanding expanded .

- **Head and Heart Knowledge**: Head knowledge involves knowing facts about theology and doctrine while heart knowledge is the kind of knowing that comes through a personal relationship and lived experience . Real faith needs both because information alone does not create a connection.

WHEN THE BIBLE BECOMES MORE THAN A BOOK

When Easy Answers Crumble

Remember how we discovered God hiding in plain sight throughout the last chapter, revealing Himself through everyday moments and ordinary experiences rather than spectacular displays? That same principle applies to how Scripture works in our lives—it rarely functions as the simple answer key we desperately want it to be.

The Bible's divine inspiration doesn't mean it functions like a spiritual vending machine where you insert a problem and receive a perfectly formatted solution. True biblical inspiration involves God working through human authors, their cultures, and their historical contexts to communicate eternal truths in ways that transcend time while remaining rooted in specific moments.

Think about it this way: when your best friend tells you something important, their personality, background, and current situation all shape how they communicate that truth to you. The same thing happens in Scripture. God didn't erase the human authors' individuality when inspiring them to write.

Key aspects of biblical inspiration include:

- Scripture contains multiple literary genres, each communicating truth through different methods—poetry doesn't function the same way as historical narrative or legal code
- Divine inspiration includes both the message and the means of communication, respecting human authors' personalities, vocabularies, and cultural contexts
- The Bible's authority comes not from magical properties in the text itself, but from its reliable testimony to God's character and His relationship with humanity

Uma learned this lesson the hard way during her junior year when she tried using Jeremiah 29:11 ("'For I know the plans I have for you,' declares the Lord, 'plans to prosper you and not to harm you'") as a guarantee that she'd get into her dream college. When the rejection letter arrived, her faith felt shattered until her mentor helped her understand that this verse was God's specific promise to Jewish exiles in Babylon, not a universal formula for personal success.

This realization didn't destroy the passage's power. It revealed something deeper.

The verse still spoke truth about God's character and His faithfulness to His people, but Uma had to wrestle with how that truth applied to her own situation rather than treating it like a magic spell. Her disappointment became an opportunity to discover that God's plans often look different from our expectations, and His definition of prosperity extends far beyond college acceptance letters.

Many teenagers experience similar frustration when they approach Scripture expecting it to solve their problems instantly. They flip through pages hunting for verses that directly address their specific situations, becoming discouraged when the Bible doesn't provide clear instructions about choosing majors, navigating relationships, or handling family conflict.

But here's what changes everything: Scripture wasn't designed to be a comprehensive life manual covering every possible scenario. Instead, it reveals the character of God and the nature of reality in ways that equip us to think wisely about situations the biblical authors never encountered.

When Frank struggled with anxiety about his future, he initially felt frustrated that the Bible didn't contain specific guidance about career choices in the twenty-first century. However, as he studied passages about God's sovereignty, human responsibility, and trusting divine provision, he developed a framework for making decisions that went far deeper than any specific instruction manual could provide.

This approach requires more work than simply finding proof texts for predetermined decisions. It demands careful study, community wisdom, and patient reflection.

But the payoff is enormous.

Rather than depending on isolated verses taken out of context, we develop the ability to think biblically about complex situations, allowing Scripture's broader themes and principles to shape our perspective on modern challenges.

This foundation prepares us for understanding even more complex theological concepts, like the Trinity, which we'll explore in our next chapter as God's ultimate plot twist that changes everything we thought we knew about divine nature.

Biblical Genres Speak Their Own Language

Just as you wouldn't read a newspaper article the same way you'd read a poem or a science textbook, the various genres within Scripture each have their own rules for communicating truth. Understanding these genres prevents misinterpretation and unlocks the intended meaning of biblical passages, building on what we learned about God's tendency to hide in plain sight through ordinary means rather than spectacular displays.

Historical Narratives: Recording Reality Without Endorsement

Historical narratives record what happened without necessarily endorsing every action they describe—David's adultery is recorded as fact, not recommended as behavior. These passages function like ancient documentaries, preserving events that reveal both human nature and God's character through real situations involving flawed people.

When Alice first read about Abraham lying about Sarah being his sister, she felt confused about whether the Bible was promoting dishonesty. Her youth pastor helped her understand that historical narratives often show us what not to do by recording the consequences of poor choices alongside examples of faithful living.

Wisdom Literature: Principles, Not Promises

Wisdom literature like Proverbs offers general principles for life rather than absolute promises—the proverbs describe how life typically works, not how it always works. These books function like collections of practical wisdom gathered from centuries of human experience and divine insight.

Consider Proverbs 22:6: "Train up a child in the way he should go, and when he is old he will not depart from it." This verse provides a general principle about parenting's long-term influence, not a guarantee that every well-raised child will automatically follow their parents' faith throughout their entire lives.

Poetry and Psalms: Emotional Truth

Biblical poetry communicates truth through imagery, emotion, and artistic expression rather than literal description. The Psalms capture the full range of human experience before God, from desperate cries for help to explosive celebrations of joy.

Psalm 137 ends with disturbing imagery about dashing babies against rocks, but understanding the genre reveals that this represents the raw emotional response of exiled people processing their grief and anger rather than God commanding infanticide.

Prophetic Literature: Divine Perspective on Current Events

Prophetic books address specific historical situations while revealing timeless truths about God's character and His relationship with humanity. These passages often contain both immediate warnings for ancient audiences and broader principles that apply across cultures and centuries.

Jacob struggled with the violent imagery in some prophetic passages until his Bible study leader explained that prophets often used dramatic metaphors to communicate the seriousness of spiritual rebellion and its consequences, similar to how modern political cartoonists use exaggerated imagery to make their points.

Apocalyptic Literature: Symbolic Truth About Spiritual Reality

Apocalyptic literature uses symbolic imagery to communicate spiritual realities that transcend literal description—Revelation's seven-headed beast isn't a biology lesson. These passages reveal God's ultimate victory over evil through vivid, sometimes bizarre imagery that captures truths too large for ordinary language.

Learning to Listen Properly

Jacob discovered this principle when he couldn't understand why Ecclesiastes seemed so depressing compared to other parts of the Bible. His small group leader explained that Ecclesiastes functions like a philosophical exploration, honestly grappling with life's apparent meaninglessness before pointing toward ultimate meaning in God.

Once Jacob understood the genre, everything changed.

He realized the book wasn't promoting nihilism—it was acknowledging the questions he'd been afraid to ask and providing a framework for finding answers. The author's honest struggle with life's difficulties made the final conclusion about fearing God and keeping His commandments more powerful, not less.

This genre awareness prepares us for understanding even more complex theological concepts. When we approach the Trinity in our next chapter, we'll discover that Scripture reveals this ultimate plot twist through multiple genres working together, each contributing unique insights that help us grasp truths about God's nature that would be impossible to communicate through any single literary approach.

When Mortals Meet the Divine Pen

The Bible's dual authorship—both human and divine—creates a beautiful complexity that enhances rather than diminishes its reliability, much like how God chose to hide in plain sight through ordinary people and everyday circumstances rather than overwhelming displays of power. God didn't override human personalities and cultural contexts; He worked through them to communicate His truth in ways that would resonate across generations.

This partnership between divine inspiration and human expression reflects the same pattern we discovered earlier: God consistently chooses to work through normal means rather than bypassing them entirely.

Understanding the Human Element

Human authors brought their unique perspectives, writing styles, and cultural backgrounds to their biblical writings, creating diversity within unity. Luke, a physician, includes medical details that other Gospel writers omit. Paul's letters reflect his rabbinical training and passionate personality. David's psalms capture the heart of a warrior-poet who understood both battlefield leadership and intimate worship.

These differences don't represent flaws in the inspiration process. They demonstrate God's intentional choice to communicate through human particularity rather than erasing individual voices.

Consider how differently Moses and Paul write about law. Moses presents detailed ceremonial regulations for ancient Israel, while Paul explains how those same principles apply to Gentile believers centuries later. Both authors address God's holiness and humanity's need for right relationship with Him, but their cultural contexts and audiences shape how they communicate these truths.

Divine Oversight Without Human Erasure

Divine inspiration ensured that despite human limitations, the essential message remained accurate and authoritative for its intended purposes. This doesn't mean every word was dictated directly by God, like some kind of supernatural dictation machine. Instead, God superintended the writing process to ensure that human authors communicated exactly what He wanted them to say, using their own vocabularies and thought patterns.

Think of it like a skilled director working with talented actors. The director ensures the story gets told correctly while allowing each performer to bring their unique gifts to their roles. The final product reflects both the director's vision and the actors' individual contributions.

Multiple Perspectives, Single Truth

This partnership model explains why the same events can be described differently in various biblical accounts without creating contradictions —different authors emphasized different aspects for different audiences. The Gospel writers provide an excellent example of this principle in action.

Brooklyn struggled with apparent contradictions between the Gospel accounts until her Bible study leader used the analogy of four friends describing the same car accident. Each witness would notice different details and emphasize different aspects based on their perspective and what they considered most important for their audience.

When she applied this understanding to the Gospels, everything clicked.

Matthew, writing primarily for Jewish readers, emphasizes how Jesus fulfills Old Testament prophecies. Mark, addressing Roman audiences, focuses on Jesus' actions and power. Luke, a Gentile physician writing for educated Greek readers, provides careful historical details and shows Jesus' concern for outcasts. John, writing later to combat false teachings, emphasizes Jesus' divine identity.

The differences between their accounts became evidence of authenticity rather than reasons for doubt. Real witnesses naturally focus on different details based on their backgrounds and purposes for telling the story.

Practical Implications

Understanding dual authorship helps us approach Scripture with appropriate expectations. We can trust the Bible's reliability while appreciating its human characteristics. We don't need to pretend that biblical authors wrote like modern historians or scientists, because God never intended them to do so.

This foundation becomes crucial as we prepare to explore the Trinity in our next chapter. The doctrine of the Trinity emerges from this same pattern of divine truth communicated through human language and categories, requiring us to embrace mystery while maintaining confidence in Scripture's trustworthy revelation of God's nature.

Scripture's GPS for Teen Crossroads

In a culture that often treats personal preference as the ultimate authority, understanding biblical authority provides teenagers with a reliable foundation for making decisions that align with reality rather than just feelings or social pressure. This authority isn't about blind obedience but about trusting a source that has proven reliable across centuries and cultures, much like how we discovered God's tendency to work through ordinary means rather than spectacular displays.

Objective Truth in a Subjective World

Biblical authority offers objective truth claims that can be tested against experience and reason, providing stability in a world of shifting cultural values. Unlike opinions that change based on current trends or personal moods, Scripture presents consistent principles about human nature, relationships, and meaning that have withstood scrutiny across diverse cultures and historical periods.

When Rosa felt pressured by her peers to compromise her values, she initially struggled because "everyone else is doing it" seemed like a compelling argument. However, understanding biblical authority helped her realize that majority opinion doesn't determine truth any more than personal preference does. The Bible's teachings about integrity and honoring God with her choices provided an anchor point that transcended social pressure.

Beyond Explicit Commands

Scripture's authority extends to both explicit commands and under-lying principles that can be applied to situations the original authors never directly addressed. The Bible doesn't contain specific instructions about social media usage, career choices, or modern dating practices, but it provides foundational principles about relationships, steward-ship, and character development that inform wise decisions in these areas.

This principle-based approach requires more thoughtful engagement than simply following a list of rules, but it equips teenagers to navigate complex situations that don't have obvious biblical precedents.

Wise Interpretation Still Required

Recognizing biblical authority doesn't eliminate the need for careful interpretation and wise application—it provides the foundation that makes such interpretation worthwhile. Understanding that Scripture carries divine authority motivates us to study it carefully, consider its historical context, and seek wisdom from mature believers who can help us apply its teachings appropriately.

Marcus faced this challenge when his friend group started experi-menting with activities that weren't explicitly forbidden in his church's rule book but didn't align with biblical principles about honoring God with his body and mind. Instead of looking for loopholes or easy answers, he learned to ask deeper questions that revealed Scripture's authority in his life.

He began asking himself important questions. What does this activity reveal about my priorities? How does it affect my relationship with God and others? What kind of person is this helping me become?

The Bible's authority gave him a framework for making decisions based on more than just "what feels right in the moment." This approach helped him understand that biblical authority isn't about restricting freedom but about providing guidance for flourishing according to God's design for human life.

Practical Application

This understanding transforms how teenagers approach major life decisions. Instead of relying solely on emotional impulses, peer pressure, or cultural expectations, they can evaluate choices against biblical principles about character, relationships, and purpose.

Biblical authority doesn't guarantee easy answers to every dilemma, but it provides a reliable reference point for navigating moral complexity. This becomes especially important during the teenage years when identity formation and decision-making skills are still developing.

Looking Forward

Understanding Scripture's nature and authority prepares us for exploring even more complex theological concepts. As we move into our next chapter about the Trinity, we'll see how this same trustworthy Scripture reveals truths about God's nature that challenge our assumptions and expand our understanding of divine reality in ways that seemed impossible until we learned to read the Bible with proper expectations and appropriate reverence for its unique authority.

Chapter 2 Toolbox: Handling the Word

- **Biblical Authority**: This is the idea that the Bible is the most reliable GPS for your life because it tells us the truth about God and how the world actually works . It acts like an anchor that keeps you steady when everyone else seems to be changing their opinions.
- **Literary Genre**: These are the different styles of writing in the Bible like poetry or history or laws. Each style has its own set of rules so you do not get confused about what the author is trying to say.
- **Dual Authorship**: This describes the partnership where God used real people with their own personalities to write the Bible while making sure the final message was exactly what He wanted us to hear .
- **Special Revelation**: While nature gives us hints about God this is the specific message where God tells us exactly who He is and what His rescue plan is through the Bible and Jesus.

THE TRINITY: GOD'S ULTIMATE PLOT TWIST

The Rich Tapestry of One God

Picture this: You're in a heated debate with your atheist friend who argues that Christianity is just another boring monotheistic religion where one lonely God sits in heaven making rules. Then you drop the Trinity bomb. Suddenly, their simple narrative crumbles as they realize they're dealing with something far more complex and fascinating than they imagined.

Remember how we discovered in Chapter 1 that God hides in plain sight, and in Chapter 2 that the Bible reveals layers upon layers of meaning? Son, and Holy Spirit. This is the ultimate plot twist that changes everything we think we know about God.

The Trinity reveals that monotheism, rather than being a simple "one God" concept, contains infinite depth and mystery. This isn't about three separate gods competing for attention like some ancient pantheon where deities fight over who gets the most worship. Instead, we're talking about one God existing in perfect relationship within Himself—a unity so rich it contains diversity without contradiction.

Think about it this way: Most people assume that "one" means simple and uncomplicated. But the Trinity shows us that divine oneness is incredibly sophisticated. It's like discovering that what you thought was a single note is actually a perfect chord with multiple harmonies creating something more beautiful than any individual sound could produce.

The Trinity defies human categories and forces us beyond simplistic thinking about the divine. When your friend claims Christianity is intellectually shallow, they're missing the point entirely. The doctrine of the Trinity has kept the brightest minds in history wrestling with its implications for centuries. It demonstrates that ultimate reality is both unified and diverse simultaneously—something that sounds impossible until you realize it perfectly explains the world we actually live in.

Look around you. Everything exists in relationship. Atoms need electrons, protons, and neutrons working together. Ecosystems require countless species interacting in complex ways. Even your own consciousness involves different parts of your brain collaborating in ways scientists still don't fully understand. The Trinity suggests that this pattern of unity-in-diversity isn't random—it's built into the very nature of reality because it reflects the character of God himself.

This complexity mirrors the sophistication we see throughout creation itself. Just as we learned that the Bible operates on multiple levels of meaning, the Trinity shows us that God's very being operates on levels we're only beginning to grasp. It's not three different personalities sharing an apartment. It's one divine essence existing eternally in three distinct persons who share perfect love, communication, and purpose.

Cole was struggling in his philosophy class when the professor claimed all monotheistic religions were "intellectually primitive." Armed with his understanding of the Trinity, he challenged this assumption by explaining how Christian monotheism actually presents the most sophisticated understanding of ultimate reality— one that accounts for both unity and diversity at the fundamental level of existence. His professor admitted he'd never considered how the Trinity completely changes the monotheism discussion, and several classmates approached Cole afterward wanting to learn more.

Here's what makes this revolutionary: The Trinity means God isn't lonely. He doesn't need creation to have relationship because perfect relationship already exists within His being. This changes everything about how we understand love, community, and purpose.

But here's the kicker—this divine community of three persons working in perfect harmony is the same God who decided to create the universe. Which brings us to our next mind-bending discovery: how this Trinitarian God approached the seemingly ordinary task of making stuff.

God's Heart Beats in Relationship

Imagine trying to explain love to someone who had lived their entire life in complete isolation. They might understand the word intellectually, but they'd miss the essential reality that love requires relationship. This is why the Trinity matters—it shows us that relationship isn't something God does; it's who God is.

Building on what we discovered about God's complex nature in the previous section, we now need to dig deeper into what this actually means for how God operates. Remember how we learned that the Bible reveals layers of meaning that transform our understanding? The Trinity does the same thing for our concept of divine love and relationship.

The Trinity reveals that God's very essence is relational. Before creation, before humans, before anything else existed, perfect love, communication, and community existed within the Godhead. This changes everything about how we think about the universe. It means relationship isn't a human invention or evolutionary accident—it's built into the fabric of reality itself.

Think about this carefully: Most religions present their gods as solitary figures who create because they're lonely or bored. But the Christian God creates from the overflow of perfect relationship. The Father, Son, and Holy Spirit have been sharing perfect love and communication for all eternity. Creation isn't God trying to fill a gap in His existence.

It's an expression of His abundant joy.

The Father, Son, and Holy Spirit demonstrate perfect unity without loss of individual identity. This isn't three people agreeing to cooperate like roommates dividing chores. Each person of the Trinity maintains distinct roles and characteristics while sharing completely in the divine essence. The Father sends, the Son obeys, the Spirit empowers—yet they remain perfectly one in purpose, will, and nature.

This divine relationship operates on a level we can barely comprehend. There's no jealousy, no competition, no miscommunication. The Father doesn't worry that the Son is getting too much attention. The Spirit doesn't feel left out when people pray to Jesus. They celebrate each other's glory because they share the same divine nature.

Divine love is not dependent on creation but flows eternally within the Trinity. This means God's love isn't conditional on having someone to love Him back. He doesn't create humans because He's emotionally needy. The Father loves the Son with perfect, infinite love, and this love has never had a beginning and will never have an end.

This explains why humans are inherently relational beings—we're made in the image of a relational God. Your deep desire for connection, your need for friendship, your longing for community—these aren't weaknesses or evolutionary leftovers. They're reflections of the Trinity stamped into your very being.

When you experience that perfect moment of connection with a friend, when you feel completely understood and accepted, you're getting a tiny glimpse of the eternal relationship that exists within God. When a family works together in harmony, when teammates support each other perfectly, when a couple loves each other selflessly, they're reflecting something of the divine community.

Florence was devastated when her parents divorced, and she began questioning whether lasting relationships were even possible. Through studying the Trinity, she discovered that perfect relationship does exist—within God Himself. This gave her hope that human relationships, while imperfect, could reflect something of that divine harmony. She realized that her longing for deep connection wasn't naive idealism but an echo of the relational nature of God within her. This understanding helped her navigate her parents' situation with both realism about human limitations and hope rooted in divine possibility.

But here's where things get really interesting: This perfectly relational God decided to create a physical universe.

Three in One, Love for All

Have you ever wondered why diversity feels so right when it's unified around a common purpose, but so wrong when it becomes divisive? A symphony orchestra captures this perfectly—different instruments, different sounds, different roles, yet creating something beautiful together. The Trinity is the ultimate model of this principle.

Think back to our discovery that the Bible operates on multiple layers of meaning, each one revealing deeper truth. The Trinity works the same way—it's not just a doctrine to memorize, but a pattern that shows up everywhere in creation and human experience. When we understand how Father, Son, and Holy Spirit relate to each other, we unlock secrets about how everything else should work too.

The Trinity provides the theological foundation for understanding how diversity and unity can coexist perfectly. This isn't some abstract theological concept that only matters in seminary classrooms. It shows us that difference doesn't threaten unity when it's grounded in love and common purpose. This has profound implications for how we view everything from church community to cultural diversity.

Consider how this plays out in the Godhead itself. The Father initiates, the Son redeems, the Spirit sanctifies. Three completely different roles, three distinct persons, yet perfect harmony. They don't compete for recognition or argue about who's most important. Each person celebrates what the others bring to their shared mission.

This gives us a revolutionary framework for human relationships and community.

True community requires both individual identity and shared commitment. The Trinity shows us that sameness isn't the goal—unity is. You don't have to become exactly like everyone else to belong. In fact, trying to eliminate differences actually weakens the whole. Just like the Father doesn't try to be the Son, and the Spirit doesn't try to be the Father, you bring something unique that can't be replaced.

But here's the key: your uniqueness has to serve something bigger than yourself. The persons of the Trinity maintain their distinct identities precisely because they're committed to their shared purpose. When your individual gifts and perspectives are offered in service of God's kingdom and the good of others, diversity becomes strength rather than division.

Diversity of gifts and perspectives strengthens rather than weakens unity. Think about your friend group. The reason you enjoy hanging out together isn't because you're all identical—it's because each person brings something different to the table. One friend is great at making people laugh, another gives wise advice, another plans amazing adventures. Your differences make the group stronger and more interesting.

The Trinity teaches us that this principle operates at every level of reality. Churches work best when they include people from different backgrounds, ages, and perspectives—all united around Christ. Communities thrive when various groups contribute their unique strengths while working toward common goals.

Love is the binding force that allows differences to complement rather than compete. This is crucial. Without love, diversity becomes chaos. With love, it becomes symphony. The Father, Son, and Spirit are held together by perfect love, which makes their differences beautiful rather than divisive.

Marcus was elected student body president at his diverse high school, where tensions between different ethnic and social groups were creating real problems. Instead of trying to minimize differences or force artificial unity, he drew on Trinitarian principles to celebrate diversity while building genuine community around shared values and goals. He organized events that highlighted different cultural contributions while emphasizing common dreams for their school. By the end of the year, the school had become a model for other districts dealing with similar challenges, and his approach earned recognition from the state education department.

Now here's where this gets really practical: This same Trinitarian God who exists in perfect diverse unity decided to create a physical world.

Trinity's Blueprint for Human Connection

Think about the best team you've ever been part of—maybe a sports team, drama production, or group project. What made it work? Likely it was people with different strengths working toward the same goal, each person valued for their unique contribution while maintaining unity of purpose. This is Trinitarian thinking in action.

Remember how we discovered that the Bible reveals layers of meaning that transform our understanding? The Trinity works the same way for human relationships. Once you grasp how Father, Son, and Holy Spirit relate to each other, you have a blueprint for every relationship in your life.

Understanding the Trinity transforms how we approach all our relationships. It gives us a model for healthy individuality within committed community, shows us how to handle disagreements without destroying unity, and provides a framework for building relationships that honor both diversity and shared purpose.

Consider how this plays out practically. In the Trinity, we see perfect authority without oppression, perfect submission without loss of dignity, and perfect equality without sameness. The Father has authority, but He doesn't lord it over the Son. The Son submits to the Father's will, but He remains fully divine. The Spirit proceeds from both, but He's not less important.

This revolutionizes how we think about leadership and authority.

Healthy relationships require both individual identity and mutual submission. You don't have to lose yourself to be in community with others. The Father doesn't stop being the Father to accommodate the Son. But each person of the Trinity also considers the others' roles and purposes in everything they do.

Apply this to your friendships. You can maintain your unique personality, interests, and perspectives while still being committed to your friends' good. You can disagree about music, movies, or even important issues without threatening your friendship—as long as your disagreements happen within a framework of love and mutual respect.

Conflict can be resolved through love-centered dialogue rather than power struggles. When the Trinity makes decisions, it's not about who can shout loudest or manipulate most effectively. It's about perfect communication rooted in perfect love. Obviously, we can't achieve that level of perfection, but we can aspire to it.

This means when you have conflicts with family members or teammates, you don't have to choose between winning and maintaining relationship. You can pursue truth and resolution while protecting the dignity of everyone involved.

Leadership should reflect the Trinity's model of authority with equality and mutual honor. The Father leads, but He doesn't diminish the Son or Spirit. True leadership serves those being led and elevates their contributions rather than building up the leader's ego.

Hope was struggling as captain of her debate team because her authoritarian approach was creating resentment among teammates. After learning about the Trinity's model of leadership—where authority exists alongside equality and mutual honor—she completely changed her style. She began valuing each team member's unique perspective while maintaining clear direction toward their goals. The team not only started winning more competitions but also became known for their supportive, collaborative culture. Other teams began asking her to share her leadership approach at tournaments.

Recap of Key Points

The Trinity isn't just abstract theology—it's God's ultimate plot twist that changes everything. Far from making monotheism boring, it reveals infinite complexity within divine unity. We've discovered that relationship is fundamental to God's nature, not an add-on, which explains why we're wired for connection. The Trinity provides the perfect model for how diversity and unity can coexist beautifully, giving us practical wisdom for building healthy communities. Most importantly, Trinitarian thinking transforms our human relationships by showing us how to honor both individual identity and committed community.

Action Steps

- This week, identify one relationship where you can apply Trinitarian principles—perhaps by celebrating someone's unique contribution while strengthening your shared commitment
- Practice explaining the Trinity to someone using the relationship and community concepts we've explored
- Look for examples where diversity and unity work together successfully

Now that we understand how the Trinity reveals God's relational nature, we're ready to tackle an even bigger question: If God is perfectly complete within Himself, why did He create anything at all?

Chapter 3 Toolbox: The God of Relationship

- **The Trinity**: This is the wild truth that our one God has always lived as a perfect three including the Father and the Son and the Holy Spirit who share a life of endless love and communication.
- **Unity in Diversity**: This is the idea that being different does not have to lead to division because just like a symphony different instruments can play together to create one incredible sound .
- **Relational Essence**: This means that God did not create us because He was lonely since He was already part of a perfect relationship and He made us because His love was so full it just overflowed .
- **Mutual Submission**: This is the no ego way the Trinity works where they honor and support one another without anyone feeling less important which gives us a blueprint for how to lead and follow in our own friendships .

THE SCANDAL OF ORDINARY CREATION

The Divine Decision to Create

Remember the Trinity we explored in the last chapter? Those three persons living in perfect harmony, complete joy, and endless love. Here's where things get really interesting. This Trinity didn't create the universe because they were bored on a cosmic Tuesday afternoon.

They weren't lonely either.

The Father, Son, and Holy Spirit already had the most amazing relationship imaginable. They shared perfect love, constant communication, and infinite joy. Nothing was missing from their divine community. They didn't need anything or anyone else to make them complete.

So why did they decide to create everything we see around us?

The answer reveals something stunning about God's character.

Creation Flows From Abundance, Not Need

Think about the last time you shared something really good with a friend. Maybe it was your favorite song, a funny video, or an amazing dessert. You didn't share it because you were missing something in your life. You shared it because the goodness was so real that you wanted someone else to experience it too.

That's closer to why God created the universe. The Trinity's love was so rich, so full, and so joyful that it naturally overflowed into creation. God made everything not to fill some divine emptiness, but to share the incredible abundance that already existed within the Godhead.

Consider these key points about divine motivation:

- God created from fullness, not emptiness
- Creation was an act of generosity, not desperation
- The universe exists because love naturally wants to expand and include others
- Every created thing is an invitation to participate in divine joy

The Generous Heart of the Creator

When we understand that creation flows from God's abundance rather than need, it completely changes how we view our existence. We're not here because God was incomplete without us. We're here because God's love is so generous that it wanted to create others who could experience and share in that divine joy.

This means your existence isn't random or accidental. God specifically chose to create you, not because the Trinity was missing something, but because they wanted to share their love with you specifically. Every person who has ever lived represents a unique way that God wanted to express divine love in the world.

A Real-Life Perspective Shift

Harrison struggled with feeling meaningless after learning about the vastness of the universe in astronomy class. The numbers were overwhelming. Billions of galaxies, each containing billions of stars. Earth seemed like a tiny speck, and his own life felt even smaller.

He brought these doubts to his youth pastor during a particularly difficult week. "If the universe is so huge, how can my life possibly matter? Am I just some cosmic accident?"

His youth pastor helped him see things differently. "The size of the universe doesn't make you insignificant. It shows how generous God is. Think about it this way - if God only wanted to share love with you, creating just Earth would have been enough. But God created this incredible, vast universe as the backdrop for your life. You're not lost in the immensity. You're the reason for it."

This conversation shifted Harrison's entire perspective. Instead of feeling lost in space, he began to feel deeply wanted. God didn't create him by accident or out of loneliness. God specifically chose to bring him into existence because the Trinity wanted to share their love with him personally.

What This Means for Us

Understanding creation as an overflow of divine love rather than divine need changes everything. It means we exist not to fill some gap in God's life, but to receive and participate in the love that already flows perfectly within the Trinity.

This truth sets up an important question we'll explore in our next chapter: if creation began so beautifully, what went wrong?

Finding Sacred in the Everyday World

Here's something that might surprise you: Christianity is one of the most physical religions in the world. While other belief systems often treat the material world as something to escape or overcome, the Trinity we discussed in the last chapter created a universe they called "very good."

Not just good. Very good.

This wasn't a consolation prize or a temporary holding pattern until something better came along. When God looked at mountains, oceans, trees, animals, and human bodies, the divine response was deep satisfaction and delight. The physical world isn't a spiritual obstacle course we need to navigate around.

It's the arena where faith comes alive.

The False Split Between Sacred and Secular

Throughout history, various groups have tried to convince people that truly spiritual individuals should focus only on "heavenly" things while treating physical reality as inferior or even evil. These ancient ideas, often called Gnostic heresies, suggested that matter was corrupt and that salvation meant escaping the physical world entirely.

This thinking still shows up today in different forms:

- "Spiritual but not religious" attitudes that dismiss organized, embodied faith communities
- Wellness culture that treats the body as something to transcend rather than steward
- Religious movements that view physical pleasure, beauty, or enjoyment as automatically suspect
- The assumption that "real" spiritual activities happen only in churches or during prayer time

But Christianity boldly rejects this false division. The same Trinity that exists in perfect relationship chose to create a material universe and declared it very good. This means your physical body, the natural world around you, and your everyday experiences all carry inherent dignity and sacred potential.

Embracing Embodied Faith

When we understand that God loves the physical world, it changes how we approach our daily lives. Suddenly, caring for our bodies becomes an act of stewardship rather than vanity. Appreciating natural beauty becomes a form of worship rather than distraction. Enjoying good food, meaningful work, and physical activities can all be ways of participating in the goodness God built into creation.

This doesn't mean everything physical is automatically spiritual. Sin has affected the material world just as it has affected our hearts. But it does mean we don't have to choose between being faithful and being fully human in a physical world.

A Story of Integration

Jade felt constantly torn between her love for hiking and photography and the message she was getting from some Christian friends that she should focus more on "spiritual" activities like Bible study and prayer. Every weekend, she faced an internal struggle: should she spend Saturday morning in the mountains with her camera, or should she attend the additional Bible study her youth group had added?

Her guilt intensified when other students made comments about prioritizing "eternal things" over "worldly hobbies." She began to wonder if her passion for outdoor photography was somehow less valuable or even spiritually harmful.

When she finally talked to her mentor about this struggle, the conversation changed everything. Her mentor explained that God created the mountains she loved to photograph and gave her eyes to see their beauty. The Trinity that spoke the world into existence also designed her specific interests and abilities.

"Your camera doesn't compete with your faith," her mentor explained. "It can be an expression of it. When you capture the beauty of creation, you're documenting God's artistry. When hiking fills you with awe and peace, you're experiencing what the Creator intended."

Jade realized that her outdoor adventures could be acts of worship, not distractions from faith. She started seeing her photography as a way of sharing God's creation with others and her hiking as time spent in the cathedral of the natural world.

The Sacred Ordinary

This understanding of creation's goodness means the sacred isn't limited to church buildings or formal religious activities. God can be encountered in art class, on the soccer field, in conversations with friends, and even in the mundane tasks of daily life.

However, this beautiful beginning raises an important question that we'll tackle in our next chapter: if creation started so good, what went so terribly wrong?

Living Mirrors of the Divine

The most shocking statement in all of creation might be this: humans are made in God's image. Not just inspired by God, influenced by God, or loved by God. Actually designed to reflect the character of the Trinity we explored in previous chapters.

This isn't just about human dignity or feeling special.

It's about having a job to do.

Being made in God's image means we're living mirrors, designed to show the world what God is like through how we live, work, create, and relate to others. This image-bearing involves both who we are and what we're called to do, giving every person incredible worth and significant responsibility.

The Components of Image-Bearing

When God created humans in the divine image, several key capacities were built into our design:

Creativity: Just as the Trinity spoke the universe into existence, humans have an innate drive to create, innovate, and bring new things into being. Whether through art, music, writing, cooking, or problem-solving, we reflect God's creative nature.

Relationship: The Trinity exists in perfect community, and humans are designed for connection. We're meant to build meaningful relationships, show love, practice forgiveness, and create communities that reflect divine unity.

Moral Responsibility: Unlike other creatures, humans can distinguish between right and wrong, make ethical choices, and be held accountable for their actions. This moral capacity reflects God's perfect justice and goodness.

Stewardship: We're given responsibility to care for creation, manage resources wisely, and protect the "very good" world God made. This isn't domination but thoughtful caretaking that reflects God's loving care for the world.

Age Doesn't Diminish the Image

Here's something important: being made in God's image isn't something you grow into or earn through good behavior. You don't become more image-bearing when you turn eighteen or graduate from high school. Teenagers carry the full dignity and responsibility of reflecting God's character right now, in your current circumstances and relationships.

This means your choices at school, your attitude at your part-time job, how you treat your siblings, and the way you handle your responsibilities all matter as expressions of God's image. You're not waiting to become significant. You're already a living representative of divine character.

Transformation in Action

When Marcus started his first job at a local restaurant, he initially saw it as just a way to earn money for a car. The work seemed meaningless: taking orders, cleaning tables, restocking supplies. He did the minimum required and counted the hours until his shift ended.

But after learning about image-bearing in youth group, his perspective completely shifted. He began to see how treating customers with respect reflected God's love for people. Working honestly, even when his manager wasn't watching, became a way to reflect divine integrity. Caring about food quality and cleanliness became expressions of the excellence that characterizes God's work.

His attitude transformation was so noticeable that his manager asked what had changed. Marcus found himself explaining that he'd started seeing his job as more than just work—it was an opportunity to show what God was like through his actions.

"I don't know what you've been learning," his manager said, "but keep it up. You've become the kind of employee every business needs."

The Weight and Wonder of It

Understanding that we're made in God's image brings both incredible dignity and serious responsibility. It means every person you encounter also bears this divine image, deserving respect and care regardless of their background, abilities, or social status.

It also means that how you live your life matters more than you might realize. You're not just making personal choices. You're representing the character of the Trinity to everyone around you.

This beautiful calling raises important questions about what happened when humanity chose to tarnish that divine image—questions we'll explore in our next chapter about the problem everyone tends to ignore.

Nurturing Life Through Creative Purpose

Before humanity fell into sin, God gave them a remarkable assignment often called the cultural mandate. This wasn't just about having dominion over creation—it was an invitation to partner with the Trinity in developing the world's potential through work, art, relationships, and innovation.

This changes everything about how we view our daily activities and future careers.

When God told humans to "fill the earth and subdue it," the Hebrew word for subdue suggests careful cultivation rather than harsh domination. Think of a gardener who doesn't destroy the natural beauty of a space but works with it to bring out its full potential. That's the kind of stewardship God had in mind.

All Work as Sacred Calling

The cultural mandate reveals that all legitimate work participates in God's ongoing creative activity. When a teacher helps students learn, they're developing human potential. When an engineer designs a bridge, they're using God-given materials and minds to solve problems and connect communities. When an artist creates beauty, they're reflecting the divine creativity we explored in earlier chapters.

This means career choices can be evaluated not just by salary or personal interest, but by how they contribute to human flourishing and creation care. Consider these examples:

- Medical professionals heal bodies, reflecting God's desire for wholeness
- Teachers and researchers develop minds and expand knowledge
- Farmers and chefs steward creation's resources to nourish people
- Artists and musicians create beauty that points to divine creativity
- Business leaders organize resources to meet human needs

None of these require explicit evangelism to be faithful expressions of Christian calling. They're all ways of participating in God's work in the world.

Environmental Responsibility as Worship

Our role as image-bearers naturally leads to environmental responsibility. If God declared creation "very good" and entrusted it to our care, then protecting ecosystems, reducing waste, and developing sustainable practices become acts of faithful obedience rather than merely political positions.

This doesn't require extreme measures or guilt-driven behavior. It means thoughtfully considering how our choices affect the world God loves and asked us to steward.

Breaking False Sacred-Secular Divisions

The cultural mandate destroys the artificial separation between "sacred" and "secular" work that many Christians unconsciously accept. The Trinity we discussed in Chapter 3 cares about all of life, not just church activities.

Consider Maya's story. She felt enormous pressure from her Christian community to go into "full-time ministry," but her heart burned with passion for marine biology. She loved studying ocean ecosystems and dreamed of working to protect marine life, yet constantly wondered if she was somehow settling for something less spiritual than pastoral work.

Learning about the cultural mandate transformed her perspective completely. She realized that studying the intricate systems God designed in our oceans was itself a form of worship. Protecting marine environments from pollution and overexploitation was caring for God's creation. Using her scientific gifts to understand and preserve ocean life was exactly the kind of stewardship God intended.

Maya discovered she could serve God through science just as faithfully as through traditional church work. Her research into coral reef restoration became her way of participating in God's care for creation.

Living Out the Mandate Today

As teenagers, you're already participating in this cultural mandate. Every time you:

- Create art, music, or writing that reflects beauty and truth
- Study diligently to develop your mind and abilities
- Care for the environment through thoughtful choices
- Build healthy relationships that reflect divine love
- Work honestly at part-time jobs
- Use technology to solve problems or connect people

You're fulfilling humanity's original calling to partner with God in developing creation's potential.

This understanding should influence how you think about your future. Instead of asking only "What career will make me happy?" or "What job pays well?" also consider "How can my gifts and interests contribute to human flourishing and creation care?"

The cultural mandate reveals that ordinary work can be extraordinary worship when done in partnership with the God who declared all creation very good.

But this beautiful calling raises troubling questions about our current world, questions we'll tackle in our next chapter.

Chapter 4 Toolbox: Making Life Count

- **Cultural Mandate**: This is the original invitation God gave us to be His partners by using our skills and hobbies to help the world grow and reach its full potential.
- **Stewardship**: Instead of just using things up this is our call to be the world's careful caretakers because God declared the physical world very good.
- **Sacred Ordinary**: This is the realization that God is just as present in your biology lab or at your part time job as He is during a Sunday service.
- **Creation from Abundance**: This means God did not create us because He was empty or bored but because He chose to be generous and share His massive joy with us

PARADISE LOST AND THE PROBLEM EVERYONE IGNORES

Our Broken Nature

Remember in Chapter 4 how we talked about the scandal of ordinary creation—how God made everything perfectly good, from towering mountains to tiny insects? and it wasn't just a minor glitch that could be fixed with better education or stricter rules.

Dominic was known as the "good kid" in his youth group—never swore, always helped with setup, memorized scripture effortlessly. But when he got to college, he found himself lying to his parents about his grades, cheating on exams, and treating his girlfriend poorly when no one was watching. His youth pastor's explanation that "sin is just breaking rules" hadn't prepared him for the reality that his heart itself was the problem.

The rules weren't broken from the outside in—the breaking came from within.

Sin as a Condition, Not Just Actions

Here's what most people get wrong about sin: they think it's like jaywalking or speeding—breaking external rules that good people occasionally mess up on. But the Bible paints a much deeper picture. Sin isn't just about individual wrong choices; it's about a fundamental brokenness in human nature that affects our desires, motivations, and capacity to choose good consistently.

Think of it like a computer virus that doesn't just corrupt individual files but affects the entire operating system. Your computer might still turn on and run programs, but everything it does is influenced by that underlying corruption. That's closer to how sin works in human beings.

We don't become sinners by sinning.

We sin because we are sinners.

This isn't just theological wordplay—it explains why even the most well-intentioned people struggle with selfishness, pride, and moral failure. Natalie might volunteer at homeless shelters every weekend, but she still finds herself gossiping about her coworkers. Her volunteer work doesn't make her a good person who occasionally slips up; rather, she's a broken person who sometimes manages to do genuinely good things despite her condition.

The Heart Problem

The Bible talks a lot about the heart, but it's not referring to that muscle pumping blood through your body. In biblical terms, the heart represents the core of who you are—your deepest desires, motivations, and the driving force behind your decisions.

Scripture says our hearts are "deceitful above all things and desperately sick." That sounds harsh, but think about it honestly. How often do you find yourself:

- Wanting credit for good things you do
- Feeling jealous when friends succeed
- Making decisions based on what others will think
- Choosing the easy path over the right path
- Putting your comfort above others' needs

These aren't just bad habits or poor choices—they reveal something deeper about human nature. Our deepest desires and motivations are skewed toward self-centeredness rather than God-centeredness. Even our good deeds often have mixed motives.

The Inability Problem

Here's perhaps the most frustrating part of human brokenness: even when we know what's right, we often lack the power to consistently do it. The apostle Paul captured this perfectly when he wrote, "I do not do the good I want, but the evil I do not want is what I keep on doing."

Dominic knew he should study instead of playing video games. Natalie knew she should forgive her sister instead of holding a grudge. But knowledge and willpower weren't enough. There's a gap between knowing what's right and having the power to do it consistently.

This isn't about being weak or lacking discipline—it's about recognizing that human beings need more than information and good intentions. We need transformation at the deepest level, something that addresses not just our actions but the very source from which those actions spring.

The problem runs deeper than we'd like to admit.

When Heroes Fall and Villains Rise

Chloe couldn't understand why her atheist biology teacher was one of the kindest, most generous people she knew, while her Christian uncle had been arrested for embezzling from his company. Her small group leader helped her see that the image of God in her teacher enabled his goodness, while her uncle's sin nature had found expression despite his faith. This understanding helped her defend Christianity when classmates pointed to "hypocritical Christians" as evidence against the faith.

If you've been following along since Chapter 4's discussion of God's perfectly good creation, you might be wrestling with some confusing observations about human behavior. Why do some non-Christians act more loving than some Christians? Why do good people sometimes do terrible things? Why do terrible people sometimes show surprising goodness?

The doctrine of sin explains this paradox better than any other worldview.

The Image That Won't Go Away

Remember how we learned that humans are created in God's image—the imago Dei that makes us different from every other creature? Here's something crucial: sin doesn't erase that image. It damages it, distorts it, corrupts it, but it doesn't destroy it completely.

Think of it like a masterpiece painting that's been damaged by fire and water. You can still see traces of the original beauty, the skilled brushwork, the artist's vision. But you can also see the damage—the blackened edges, the faded colors, the torn canvas. That's closer to what happened to humanity.

Even the worst people retain dignity and capacity for good because they're made in God's image. This explains why Brandon was shocked to discover that his neighbor, who had spent years in prison, was the first person to help when his family faced a crisis. The image of God in that man hadn't disappeared—it was still there, still capable of expressing itself in moments of genuine goodness.

Total Depravity Doesn't Mean Utter Depravity

Theologians use the term "total depravity" to describe human sinfulness, but this creates confusion. It doesn't mean we're as bad as we could possibly be—that would be "utter depravity." Instead, total depravity means we're affected by sin in every area of our being.

Picture it this way: if sin were like ink dropped into water, total depravity would mean the ink has colored every drop of water, not that the water has turned completely black. Our minds, emotions, will, and relationships all bear sin's influence, but we're not utterly evil in every possible way.

This explains why Chloe could write beautiful poetry that reflected truth and beauty, even though she rejected God. The image of God in her enabled that creativity and insight, even while sin distorted other areas of her life.

Common Grace Changes Everything

Here's where things get really interesting. God doesn't just save some people and abandon everyone else to complete moral chaos. Through what theologians call "common grace," God restrains evil and enables good even in people who don't believe in him.

Common grace works through several channels:

- Conscience: That inner voice that tells right from wrong
- Social structures: Laws, customs, and expectations that promote order
- Natural law: Built-in understanding of basic moral principles
- Relationships: Family bonds and community connections that encourage good behavior

This is why secular governments can establish just laws, why non-Christian doctors can heal the sick with genuine compassion, and why atheist teachers can show remarkable kindness to their students. God's grace is working in their lives, not to save them eternally, but to restrain evil and promote human flourishing.

Making Sense of Moral Complexity

Understanding both the image of God and total depravity helps us navigate moral complexity without becoming cynical or naive. We can appreciate genuine goodness wherever we find it while remaining realistic about human nature's bent toward selfishness and sin.

This sets us up perfectly for what's coming in Chapter 6—the impossible rescue mission that addresses both our retained dignity and our desperate need.

Human nature is more complex than simple categories allow.

When Personal Choices Ripple Outward

Marcus grew up in a small town where "everyone knew" that certain families were "no good" and certain neighborhoods were "rough." When he studied his town's history for a school project, he discovered that discriminatory lending practices from the 1950s had created the economic conditions that led to the current problems. Individual racist choices by bank officers decades ago had created systems that were still hurting people today. This helped him understand why the Bible talks about sin affecting "the third and fourth generation."

We've been talking about sin as something that happens inside individual hearts—the broken nature we discussed earlier in this chapter. But here's what makes sin even more complicated: it doesn't stay inside individual hearts. Like ripples spreading across a pond, personal sinful choices create waves that affect entire communities, cultures, and generations.

Sin isn't just personal—it's corporate.

How Individual Choices Build Broken Systems

Think about how systems get started. Someone with power makes a decision based on selfishness, fear, or prejudice. Maybe a business owner in the 1960s decides not to hire people from certain ethnic backgrounds. That individual choice seems small at the time, but it creates a pattern. Other business owners follow suit, either because they share the prejudice or because they don't want to rock the boat.

Fast forward sixty years, and you have entire communities where certain groups have been systematically excluded from economic opportunities. The original prejudiced business owners might be dead, but their choices created systems that outlast them. Young people today inherit the consequences of decisions they never made.

This isn't just about racism—though that's a clear example. Consider how individual choices to prioritize profits over employee wellbeing can create corporate cultures that treat workers as disposable. Or how individual decisions to ignore environmental damage can create systems that poison entire watersheds for generations.

Your choices don't just affect you. They contribute to the moral atmosphere around you and can make it easier or harder for others to choose good.

When Sin Becomes Normal

Here's something even more subtle: communities develop accepted ways of sinning that feel completely normal to the people living in them. These cultural sin patterns become so embedded that people stop noticing they're problems.

Consider the high school where gossip is the primary form of social bonding. New students quickly learn that sharing rumors and talking behind people's backs is how you fit in. Nobody sits down and decides to create a "gossip culture"—it just emerges from thousands of individual choices to prioritize social status over kindness.

Or think about communities where materialism runs so deep that people go into debt to keep up appearances, where success is measured only by possessions, where relationships are valued based on what someone can provide. These patterns feel normal to people living inside them, but they're actually corporate expressions of individual sinful choices multiplied across entire populations.

Rachel noticed this when she moved from her small rural town to a wealthy suburb. In her old community, modesty and contentment were valued. In her new school, constantly wanting more—better clothes, newer phones, fancier cars—was just expected. The sin pattern of her new community made it much harder for her to practice contentment.

The Generational Legacy

Perhaps the most sobering aspect of corporate sin is how it gets passed down through families and communities. Parents who grew up in broken systems often unconsciously pass those patterns to their children, not because they're bad people, but because it's all they know.

A father who learned to handle conflict through anger passes that pattern to his son. A mother who was taught that her worth depends on her appearance passes that insecurity to her daughter. Communities that normalized certain prejudices pass those attitudes to the next generation through countless small interactions and assumptions.

This generational impact explains why some problems seem so persistent, why changing individual hearts isn't always enough to fix systemic issues.

But understanding corporate sin also sets up our hope for what's coming in Chapter 6—a rescue mission that addresses not just individual hearts but entire broken systems.

Born Guilty or Self-Made Choices

Sophia struggled with this concept when her friend was arrested for drunk driving after hitting another car. Was her friend a victim of the alcoholism that ran in his family, or was he fully responsible for choosing to drink and drive? Her pastor helped her see that both could be true: her friend's family history made his struggle with alcohol more likely and more difficult, but he was still responsible for his choice to get behind the wheel. This understanding helped her show both compassion and appropriate accountability.

One of the most challenging questions in all of theology is this: Are we born guilty, or do we make ourselves guilty through our choices? It's tempting to pick one side or the other, but the biblical picture requires us to hold both truths at the same time.

This creates tension, but it's the kind of tension that leads to wisdom.

The Condition We Inherit

From the moment you drew your first breath, you inherited something you didn't choose: a sin nature. This isn't about specific sins you've committed—it's about the fundamental orientation of your heart toward self-centeredness rather than God-centeredness.

Think about how babies behave. They don't need lessons in selfishness. A two-year-old doesn't share toys naturally—she has to be taught. Children don't automatically tell the truth when it might get them in trouble. Nobody teaches kids to be jealous of their siblings' attention or to want what belongs to others.

This inherited condition makes us inclined toward selfishness and rebellion against God. It's like being born with a compass that points slightly off true north—every step you take leads you further from your intended destination, even when you think you're going the right way.

Lucas noticed this when his baby sister was born. Everyone called her "innocent," but even as an infant, she seemed to instinctively know how to manipulate adults to get what she wanted. She wasn't evil, but she wasn't neutral either.

The Choices We Make

But here's where it gets complicated: despite our inherited condition, we remain responsible for our individual decisions and actions. We're not robots programmed to sin without any real choice in the matter.

Every day, you face genuine decisions between right and wrong, selfishness and love, truth and deception. Your sin nature makes choosing good more difficult and choosing evil more appealing, but it doesn't eliminate your ability to choose. When you lie to your parents, cheat on a test, or treat someone cruelly, you're making a real choice that you're responsible for.

Consider how different people with similar backgrounds make vastly different choices. Two siblings growing up in the same broken home might respond completely differently—one might become bitter and destructive, while the other develops unusual compassion and resilience.

Both/And Thinking

The key is learning to hold both truths simultaneously: we're victims of a condition beyond our control AND responsible agents who make real choices. This "both/and" thinking prevents us from two dangerous extremes.

On one side, we avoid the trap of fatalism—the idea that we're doomed to sin and can't help ourselves. That kind of thinking removes personal responsibility and makes real change impossible.

On the other side, we avoid the trap of moralism—the idea that we're basically good people who just need to try harder. That kind of thinking ignores the deep heart problem that makes consistent goodness impossible through willpower alone.

Maya learned this balance when working with kids in foster care. Their traumatic backgrounds explained many of their behavioral problems and helped her respond with compassion instead of judgment. But she also had to maintain clear boundaries and expectations, because treating them as if they had no choice would have been another form of harm.

Living in the Tension

This tension between inherited sinfulness and personal accountability creates one of theology's most complex discussions, but understanding both elements is crucial for a balanced worldview that neither excuses evil nor crushes people under impossible expectations.

When someone you care about makes destructive choices, you can have compassion for their struggles while still holding them accountable for their actions. When you fail morally, you can acknowledge your responsibility without falling into despair about your inherent brokenness.

Understanding this balance prepares us for the impossible rescue mission we'll explore next.

When Nature Goes Rogue

If God is good and He is in control, then why do we have to deal with things like tsunamis or earthquakes or kids born with cancer? This is the exact question that stopped Cole in his tracks and it is one we have to face head on.

When we talked about sin earlier, we described it as a virus in the human heart. But the Bible suggests that when humanity turned away from God, it was like the entire operating system of the universe got a glitch. We live in a world that is currently a paradise lost. This means that the physical world including the weather and the ground and even our own DNA does not always function the way God originally intended it to.

The Bible says that creation itself is groaning like it is in labor as it waits for the day God fixes everything. Natural disasters and illnesses are not God being mean. They are symptoms of a world that is currently broken and waiting for its ultimate renovation.

The unshakeable faith Cole eventually found was not based on ignoring these tragedies. Instead, it was based on knowing that God is not indifferent to them. In the middle of the mess, we have a God who entered into the pain through Jesus. He is someone who knows what it is like to suffer and lose a friend. He is not just watching from the sidelines. He is the one who has already promised to one day end every disease and wipe away every single tear.

Chapter 5 Toolbox: Facing the Brokenness

- **Total Depravity**: Think of this as a system wide virus that has affected every single part of being human including our minds and our emotions . It does not mean we are as bad as we could possibly be but it does mean that sin has touched every area of our lives .
- **Common Grace**: This is the kindness of God that keeps the world from falling into total moral chaos . It is the reason why people who do not believe in God can still be kind and do amazing things like heal the sick or create beautiful art .
- **Corporate Sin**: This describes how sin ripples outward and does not just stay in our own hearts . It explains how individual selfish choices can build up over time to create broken systems and cultural patterns that hurt people for generations .
- **The Heart Problem**: In the Bible the heart represents the mission control center of who you are including your deepest desires and motivations . Because our hearts are naturally bent toward ourselves rather than God we need a transformation that goes deeper than just following more rules.

THE IMPOSSIBLE RESCUE MISSION

The Divine-Human Mystery of Jesus

Picture yourself trapped at the bottom of a deep well with no way to climb out. The walls are too slippery, too high, and you're getting weaker by the hour. Someone wants to rescue you, but they face a complex problem that requires a very specific solution.

Your rescuer needs two essential qualities that seem to contradict each other.

First, they must be able to reach down to where you are. They need to understand your exact situation, feel the cold water around your ankles, and know the panic that sets in when you realize you can't save yourself. They need to be human enough to actually connect with your experience.

Second, they must be strong enough to pull you up. They need power that goes beyond normal human strength, authority that can command the very forces keeping you trapped, and the ability to lift you completely out of danger. They need to be divine enough to actually accomplish the rescue.

This is exactly why Jesus needed to be both fully human and fully divine. Anything less would have made the rescue mission impossible.

The Human Side of the Mission

Jesus didn't just pretend to be human like an actor putting on a costume for a play. He became fully human in every way that matters, experiencing everything we experience except sin itself. He felt hunger when he hadn't eaten, exhaustion when he worked long days, and genuine sorrow when his friend Lazarus died.

When we read about Jesus being tempted in the wilderness for forty days, this wasn't some cosmic theater production where God was just going through the motions. Jesus felt real hunger, real weakness, and real temptation. He understood what it meant to want something that seemed easier than doing the right thing.

Only as fully human could Jesus truly represent humanity before God.

The Divine Side of the Mission

But being human wasn't enough for the rescue mission Jesus came to accomplish. The problems we explored in Chapter 5 - our broken relationship with God, our tendency toward selfishness, and the reality of death itself - required solutions that no ordinary human could provide.

Jesus needed divine power to forgive sins, divine authority to command storms and raise the dead, and divine nature to bridge the gap between holy God and sinful humanity. When Jesus said "I and the Father are one," he wasn't speaking metaphorically. He was claiming the divine nature necessary to complete the impossible rescue.

Only as fully divine could Jesus possess the power to break chains that no mere human could overcome.

The Perfect Bridge

Nathan was struggling with depression during his junior year, feeling like God was too distant to understand what he was going through. His youth pastor explained how Jesus, as fully human, experienced deep sorrow in the Garden of Gethsemane. The stress was so intense that Luke records Jesus sweating drops of blood - a real medical condition called hematidrosis that happens under extreme emotional pressure.

But his youth pastor also reminded Nathan that Jesus, as fully divine, had the power to transform that suffering into hope and healing.

This helped Nathan realize something profound. God wasn't standing at a safe distance from his pain, offering advice from the sidelines. Instead, God had entered completely into human experience while maintaining the divine power necessary to bring real change.

What This Means for the Rescue

The union of divine and human natures in Jesus means he serves as the perfect mediator between God and humanity. He can represent us to God because he's one of us. He can represent God to us because he's fully divine.

This sets up the great exchange we'll explore next.

When God Chose Flesh Over Distance

When a CEO visits a struggling factory, they might tour the facility, shake some hands, and give an encouraging speech from a safe distance. But imagine if instead, the CEO sold their mansion, moved into the factory town, worked on the assembly line for years, and made the workers' struggles their own daily reality. This radical choice would send a completely different message about how much the company and its people actually matter.

This is what the incarnation represents - not God visiting creation like a distant executive, but God moving in permanently and sharing our experience from the inside.

The Ultimate Investment Decision

Think about the broken world we explored in Chapter 5. Humanity had chosen rebellion over relationship with God, creating a massive gap between the holy God and his creation. The obvious solution might have been for God to maintain his distance and work through messengers, signs, or supernatural interventions from heaven.

Instead, God made the most shocking investment decision in history.

He chose to become permanently part of the very creation that had rejected him. Not temporarily, not as a brief visit, but forever. When the Word became flesh, as John puts it, this wasn't a short-term assignment with a return ticket to heaven. This was God choosing to join the human race permanently.

What This Choice Reveals

The incarnation demonstrates that creation isn't disposable to God but so valuable that he was willing to become part of it forever. When something is truly precious to you, you don't keep it at arm's length. You draw it close, invest in it deeply, and make its concerns your own concerns.

Through taking on human nature permanently, God shows that the physical world and human experience have eternal significance and dignity. Your body isn't just a temporary shell for your soul. Your daily struggles aren't just inconveniences to endure until you get to heaven. Your relationships, your work, your creativity, even your need for food and sleep - all of these have eternal importance because God chose to experience them himself.

This divine commitment transforms how we view our own lives and the world around us.

The Personal Impact

Penelope was going through a particularly difficult time when her parents divorced. She felt like God had abandoned her family, leaving them to figure out custody schedules, divided holidays, and the awkward reality of choosing sides. Her small group leader explained that in the incarnation, God didn't just send help from a distance - he became permanently invested in human experience, including family pain and brokenness.

Understanding that God had literally joined the human family and experienced its complexities helped Penelope see her situation differently. This wasn't evidence of God's absence, but something God cared about deeply enough to enter personally.

Beyond Temporary Solutions

The incarnation reveals God's long-term strategy for dealing with the problems we explored earlier. Instead of offering quick fixes or temporary patches, God chose to address human brokenness by becoming human himself. This wasn't a brief intervention but a permanent commitment to sharing our condition.

When Jesus experienced hunger, he wasn't just checking a box on his earthly to-do list. He was permanently joining the ranks of those who know what empty stomachs feel like. When he felt the sting of rejection, he wasn't gathering research for a divine report. He was becoming forever part of the human experience of being misunderstood.

Setting Up the Exchange

This permanent investment in human nature sets the stage for something even more remarkable. God didn't just choose to experience our condition - he chose to do something about it from the inside. The rescue mission we've been exploring required not just divine power from above, but divine presence within human experience itself.

The great exchange that follows depends entirely on this fundamental choice.

Beyond the Cross to Daily Grace

Most rescue stories focus on the dramatic final moment - the hero bursting through to save the day in a blaze of glory. But Jesus' rescue mission was more like a master craftsman spending years creating a perfect key that could unlock every door that trapped humanity. His entire life was the forging of that key, with each experience adding another essential element to our salvation.

We often think the cross was the only part that mattered, but that misses the bigger picture of how salvation actually works.

The Lifelong Project of Righteousness

Remember the problems we explored in Chapter 5 - humanity's broken relationship with God and our inability to live up to his standards. Jesus didn't just die to remove our guilt. His perfect obedience throughout his entire life provided the righteousness that humanity lacked, not just removing our guilt but clothing us in his goodness.

Every time Jesus chose obedience over convenience, every moment he resisted temptation, every act of compassion he showed - all of this was actively building the righteousness that would become ours. When he was twelve years old and stayed behind in the temple because he needed to be about his Father's business, that wasn't just a cute childhood story. That was righteousness being forged.

When he spent forty days in the wilderness saying no to Satan's temptations, he wasn't just proving a point. He was earning the perfect record that Adam and Eve had lost and that we desperately needed.

Revealing What God Actually Looks Like

Jesus' teachings and miracles revealed God's character and kingdom, showing us what restored relationship with God actually looks like in practice. The people in his time had been hearing about God through rules, regulations, and religious systems. But Jesus showed them what God was actually like by being God among them.

When Jesus touched lepers instead of avoiding them, he revealed that God doesn't find us disgusting in our brokenness. When he welcomed children while the disciples tried to shoo them away, he showed that God delights in those the world considers unimportant. When he ate with tax collectors and sinners, he demonstrated that God's love reaches the people religious folks write off.

Each miracle wasn't just a random display of power but a window into God's heart for his creation.

The Daily Template for Living

Jesus' resistance to temptation and faithful endurance through suffering demonstrated how to live as God intended, providing both example and empowerment for our own spiritual growth. His life gives us a template for what human life looks like when it's properly connected to God.

Marcus used to think that only Jesus' death mattered for salvation, which made him feel like the rest of Jesus' story was just interesting background information. The Sermon on the Mount was inspiring, the parables were clever, and the miracles were impressive, but the real action happened at the cross.

But when his pastor explained how Jesus' entire life was actively saving humanity - his obedience earning righteousness, his teachings revealing truth, his compassion modeling love - Marcus realized he could look to every part of Jesus' life for guidance and strength.

This transformed Marcus's Bible reading from focusing only on the crucifixion to finding salvation's power throughout the Gospels.

The Complete Solution

Jesus' life wasn't just the warm-up act before the main event. Every word he spoke, every choice he made, and every relationship he built was part of the comprehensive solution to humanity's comprehensive problem. His active obedience earned what we needed, while his passive obedience on the cross paid what we owed.

This sets us up to understand the remarkable exchange that makes salvation possible.

One Life That Changed Everything

It seems almost unfair, doesn't it? If God wanted to save everyone, why not appear to every culture simultaneously? Why choose one specific person, in one small region, at one particular moment in history? This "scandal of particularity" bothers many people, but it actually reveals something profound about how real change happens - through specific, concrete actions rather than vague universal principles.

Why Specificity Matters

God works through particular people and events because real relationships and genuine transformation require specificity, not abstract concepts. Think about the most meaningful relationships in your life. They didn't develop through general principles about friendship or love. They formed through specific conversations, shared experiences, and concrete acts of care that happened at particular times and places.

When your best friend helped you through that difficult breakup, they didn't send you a philosophical essay about healing. They showed up at your house with ice cream and listened to you cry. The specificity of their actions made the comfort real.

Similarly, God's love isn't just a nice idea floating around the universe. It took concrete form in a specific person who lived in a particular place, spoke specific words, and performed real actions that people could witness and touch.

Making Salvation Concrete

The historical specificity of Jesus makes salvation concrete and verifiable rather than just a nice idea or philosophical concept. We can point to actual events that happened in real time and space. Jesus was born during Caesar Augustus's reign, grew up in Nazareth, ministered in Galilee and Judea, and was crucified under Pontius Pilate.

This isn't mythology or abstract spirituality. These are historical events that can be investigated, discussed, and verified through the same methods we use to study any other historical figure.

From One to Many

Abigail was challenged by a friend who asked why God would choose to reveal himself through one religion instead of all religions equally. At first, Abigail felt defensive and wasn't sure how to respond. The question seemed to suggest that Christianity's claims were somehow unfair or narrow-minded.

But after discussing it with her mentor, she realized that her friend's own life showed the same pattern. He had one specific family, attended one particular school, and had been shaped by specific experiences and relationships. Yet these particular influences helped him connect with people from all backgrounds and cultures.

This helped Abigail explain how God's specific action in Jesus was designed to reach every person and culture, just like how specific acts of love in families create people capable of loving others broadly.

From this one particular person and moment, the message spreads to all cultures and times, showing how God often works through the specific to reach the universal. A single stone dropped in a pond creates ripples that eventually reach every shore.

The Pattern of God's Work

Throughout the Bible, we see this same pattern. God didn't speak to everyone at once but chose specific people like Abraham, Moses, and David. He didn't establish his presence everywhere simultaneously but chose one particular people and one specific place for his temple. Yet through these particular choices, his influence spread to bless all nations.

Jesus represents the culmination of this pattern - one life that would change everything for everyone.

Setting Up the Exchange

This specificity sets up something remarkable. Because Jesus lived one perfect human life, accumulating righteousness through specific choices and actions, he created something that could be shared with everyone who believes in him.

The great exchange we'll explore next depends entirely on this one life lived perfectly in our place.

Chapter 6 Toolbox: The God Who Showed Up

- **Incarnation**: This is the incredible fact that God did not stay at a distance. He actually chose to become human and move into our world permanently to share our daily reality .
- **Mediator**: Because Jesus is both fully God and fully human He is the perfect bridge who can represent us to God and God to us .

- **Active Obedience**: Jesus did more than just die for us. He lived a life of perfect obedience every single day to earn the righteous record that we needed but could never achieve on our own.
- **Scandal of Particularity**: This is the idea that God chose to save the whole world through one specific person in one tiny part of history. It shows that real love happens through specific actions and relationships rather than just big abstract ideas.

THE GREAT EXCHANGE NOBODY TALKS ABOUT

The Beautiful Complexity of Christ's Sacrifice

Ian stood in his youth pastor's office, frustrated tears threatening to spill over. "I don't get it," he said. "My friend says Jesus died to pay for our sins, but my grandmother always talks about Jesus defeating Satan. My theology teacher mentioned something about Jesus being our perfect example. Which one is right?" His youth pastor smiled gently. "What if I told you they all are?"

The cross of Christ is like a magnificent diamond with multiple facets —each angle reveals a different aspect of its beauty, but you need to see them all to appreciate the whole gem. For centuries, Christians have developed various models to understand what Jesus accomplished through his death and resurrection, not because one explanation is insufficient, but because the reality is so rich that multiple perspectives are needed to grasp its full meaning.

The Major Models of Atonement:

- The substitutionary model emphasizes Christ taking our place and bearing our punishment

- The Christus Victor model focuses on Christ's victory over sin, death, and Satan
- The moral influence model highlights how Christ's love transforms us and calls us to follow his example
- Each model addresses different aspects of the human condition and reveals different dimensions of God's character

Hannah discovered this truth during her sophomore year when she was struggling with both guilt over past mistakes and fear about her future. She found that understanding Christ as both her substitute (dealing with guilt) and her victor over fear (conquering the powers that enslaved her) gave her a more complete foundation for her faith. When her philosophy teacher challenged the "primitive" idea of substitutionary atonement, she was able to explain how this was just one facet of a much richer theological diamond, demonstrating both intellectual sophistication and deep faith.

The substitutionary model, rooted in passages like Isaiah 53 and 2 Corinthians 5:21, addresses our guilt problem by showing how Christ bore the penalty for our sins, satisfying God's justice while expressing his love. This isn't about an angry God needing to hurt someone—it's about a loving God taking the consequences of sin upon himself rather than leaving us to bear them alone.

The Christus Victor model, emphasized by early church fathers and passages like Colossians 2:15, reveals how Christ defeated the spiritual powers that hold humanity captive. When Jesus died and rose again, he broke the power of sin, death, and Satan's accusations against us. This model speaks to our powerlessness against forces bigger than ourselves.

It's not either-or, it's both-and.

The moral influence model, while sometimes oversimplified, captures the transformative power of Christ's sacrificial love. When we truly grasp what God did for us, it changes how we live and love others. This model addresses our motivational problem—we need inspiration and example to live differently.

Building on Chapter 6's impossible rescue mission theme, we see that the rescue wasn't just about getting us out of danger—it involved a complete exchange. Christ took our sin, death, and condemnation while giving us his righteousness, life, and acceptance. The theological term for this is "substitution," but it's more beautiful than any technical word can capture.

This great exchange also sets up what we'll explore in Chapter 8 about resurrection. Death couldn't hold Jesus because he had no sin of his own—he was only carrying ours temporarily. His victory over death becomes our victory, completing the exchange he began on the cross.

Understanding these multiple dimensions helps us avoid theological tunnel vision. When someone challenges one model, we don't need to defend just that single perspective. Instead, we can acknowledge the complexity and richness of what Christ accomplished.

The cross reveals God's justice, love, power, and wisdom simultaneously. That's why it's been captivating minds and changing hearts for two thousand years.

Four Paths to Understanding Atonement

When Marcus tried to explain to his skeptical lab partner why he believed in Christianity, he found himself stumbling over theological jargon that made little sense outside church walls. "It's like Jesus paid a debt or something," he mumbled, realizing how inadequate his explanation sounded. Later that week, his youth leader helped him understand these concepts in ways that connected to real life.

These four major theories of atonement each address fundamental human needs and experiences that every person can understand, regardless of their religious background. Rather than competing explanations, they work together like instruments in an orchestra, each contributing its unique voice to a beautiful symphony of redemption.

The Four Classical Models:

- Substitution theory: Christ takes our place in judgment, like

someone paying your court fine or serving your prison
sentence

- Victory theory: Christ defeats the powers that enslave us—sin,
death, fear, and evil—like a liberating army freeing prisoners
of war
- Example theory: Christ shows us what perfect love looks like
and inspires us to follow, like a mentor who models the life we
want to live
- Satisfaction theory: Christ restores the honor and relationship
broken by sin, like someone making amends for a wrong that
damaged a friendship

Sarah used these everyday analogies when her college roommate
asked about her faith. Instead of using churchy language, she
explained how she had experienced all four realities: freedom from
guilt (substitution), victory over her anxiety disorder (victory), inspiration to serve others (example), and restored relationship with God (satisfaction). Her roommate, who had never shown interest in spiritual
things, found herself genuinely curious about a faith that addressed
such practical, universal human experiences.

The substitution model speaks to our legal problem. When we break
God's moral law, we face consequences—just like breaking civil laws
brings penalties. Christ stepped in as our substitute, taking the punishment we deserved so we could go free. This isn't about God being
mean or needing to hurt someone. It's about justice being satisfied
while mercy triumphs.

Justice and mercy meet at the cross.

The victory model addresses our power problem. We're not just guilty;
we're enslaved. Sin, death, Satan, and fear have real power over
human lives. Christ didn't just pay a penalty—he won a war. His death
and resurrection broke the chains that bind us, setting captives free
from forces too strong for us to overcome alone.

The example model tackles our inspiration problem. Even if we're
forgiven and freed, we still need to know how to live. Christ's life and

death show us what perfect love looks like in action. His sacrifice inspires us to love others sacrificially and gives us a pattern to follow.

The satisfaction model handles our relationship problem. Sin doesn't just make us guilty criminals or enslaved victims—it makes us dishonoring rebels who have damaged our relationship with God. Christ's perfect obedience and sacrifice restore God's honor while making reconciliation possible.

Building on Chapter 6's impossible rescue mission, we see that the rescue required multiple solutions because we had multiple problems. A simple "get out of jail free" card wouldn't address our need for victory, inspiration, and restored relationship.

These models also prepare us for Chapter 8's exploration of resurrection. Death couldn't hold Christ because his sacrifice was complete and perfect. His victory over death validates every aspect of his atoning work and guarantees our future resurrection.

Understanding all four models helps us communicate more effectively with different people. Some respond to legal language about substitution. Others connect better with victory imagery. Still others find inspiration in Christ's moral example or restoration language about relationships.

The beauty lies in the combination.

Together, these models reveal the incredible richness of what Christ accomplished. We don't have to choose just one perspective when the reality encompasses them all.

Christ's Answer to Life's Deepest Wounds

Derek had always thought the gospel was mainly about forgiveness of sins, until his counselor helped him realize that his real struggle wasn't guilt—it was shame. "Guilt says 'I did something bad,'" she explained. "Shame says 'I am something bad.' They need different kinds of healing." This conversation opened his eyes to how the cross addresses not just one human problem, but the full spectrum of what keeps us from flourishing.

The human condition involves multiple layers of brokenness that can't all be solved the same way. Christ's work on the cross is comprehensive, addressing each dimension of our alienation and need with specific, targeted healing that gets to the root of our deepest struggles.

The Four Deep Wounds:

- Guilt (what we've done wrong) is addressed through substitution and forgiveness
- Shame (who we believe we are) is healed through our new identity as beloved children of God
- Fear (what might happen to us) is conquered through Christ's victory over death and evil powers
- Meaninglessness (why our lives matter) is answered through our participation in God's cosmic restoration project

Rachel realized the power of this comprehensive salvation when she was working with middle school students at her church. One student struggled with guilt over lying to his parents, another with shame about her family's financial struggles, a third with fear about his parents' divorce, and a fourth with meaninglessness after her grandfather's death. She was amazed to discover that the gospel had specific good news for each situation—not generic comfort, but targeted healing that addressed the particular type of brokenness each student was experiencing.

Guilt demands justice.

When we've done wrong, our conscience accuses us and demands punishment. The substitutionary aspect of Christ's work directly addresses this need. He took our punishment so we could receive forgiveness. This isn't about bypassing justice—it's about justice being fully satisfied through Christ's sacrifice.

Shame cuts deeper than guilt because it attacks our identity. Shame tells us we're fundamentally flawed, unlovable, and worthless. But through the cross, God declares us his beloved children. We don't just get forgiven actions—we get a new identity. Christ's righteousness becomes ours, transforming how we see ourselves.

Fear paralyzes us with threats of future harm.

The victory model of atonement directly confronts our deepest fears. Christ defeated death, the ultimate fear that haunts human existence. He also conquered Satan, whose accusations fuel our anxieties. When we know that the worst thing that could happen to us (death) has been defeated, other fears lose their power.

Meaninglessness whispers that our lives don't matter in the vast scope of history. But Christ's work reveals that we're part of God's grand story of restoration. Our lives have cosmic significance because we participate in healing the world's brokenness. This isn't about earning meaning through good works—it's about discovering the meaning already built into our existence.

Building on Chapter 6's impossible rescue mission, we see that the rescue had to be this comprehensive because the damage was this complete. A partial solution wouldn't have been sufficient for the depth of human need.

This multi-dimensional healing also sets up Chapter 8's discussion of resurrection. Christ's resurrection proves that his victory over guilt, shame, fear, and meaninglessness is complete and permanent. Death couldn't hold him because he had truly conquered every aspect of what separates us from life.

Understanding these different dimensions helps us minister more effectively to others and apply the gospel more specifically to our own lives. When someone is struggling with shame, quoting verses about forgiveness might miss the mark. When someone is paralyzed by fear, they need to hear about Christ's victory.

The cross is comprehensive medicine for comprehensive brokenness.

This is why the great exchange is so beautiful—Christ didn't just trade his righteousness for our sin. He traded his identity for our shame, his courage for our fear, and his purpose for our meaninglessness.

Redemption Reaches Beyond Personal Boundaries

Emma had grown up thinking that salvation was primarily about "getting into heaven when you die," until her environmental science class made her wonder what God thought about the destruction of creation. When she brought this question to her small group leader, she was surprised to learn that the Bible talks about the redemption of all creation, not just individual souls.

The cross accomplishes something far grander than personal fire insurance—it initiates the restoration of the entire cosmos. This cosmic perspective transforms how we understand our purpose in the world and gives weight and dignity to every aspect of human life and culture.

The Scope of Redemption:

- Creation itself will be liberated from decay and corruption (Romans 8:19-22)
- Human systems, cultures, and institutions can be redeemed and transformed
- Our work, relationships, creativity, and stewardship matter eternally, not just our "spiritual" activities
- The gospel has implications for justice, beauty, truth, and flourishing in every sphere of life

Tyler discovered this truth when he was considering his major in college. He had assumed that only "ministry" careers really mattered to God, but learning about the cosmic scope of redemption helped him see that his passion for sustainable engineering could be a genuine calling. He realized that working to heal environmental damage was participating in the same redemptive work that Christ began on the cross—bringing restoration to a broken world. This understanding gave him confidence to pursue his studies with the same sense of purpose he had previously reserved for church activities.

This cosmic view of redemption connects directly to Chapter 4's discussion of creation's original goodness. The physical world isn't something we escape from—it's something God plans to restore. When

Christ died and rose again, he didn't just save souls; he began the process of making all things new.

The creation groans, waiting for restoration.

Romans 8 tells us that creation itself suffers under the curse of sin, waiting eagerly for redemption. This means environmental care, urban planning, medical research, education reform, and artistic expression can all be forms of Christian discipleship when done with redemptive intent.

Building on Chapter 6's impossible rescue mission, we see that the rescue includes not just humans but the entire created order. The mission wasn't to evacuate people from a doomed planet but to reclaim and restore God's good world from the effects of the fall.

This understanding revolutionizes how we think about careers, hobbies, and daily activities. A teacher participating in God's redemptive work through education. An artist reflecting God's creativity and beauty. A businessperson creating flourishing through ethical commerce. A parent nurturing the next generation.

Every good thing points toward ultimate restoration.

When we experience beauty in music, satisfaction in meaningful work, or joy in relationships, we're tasting the reality that Christ's redemptive work is moving toward. These experiences are previews of the fully restored world to come.

This cosmic scope also prepares us for Chapter 8's discussion of resurrection. Christ's bodily resurrection proves that physical reality matters to God and will be renewed, not discarded. His resurrection is the first fruit of creation's ultimate restoration.

Understanding redemption this way helps us avoid the sacred-secular divide that plagues many Christians. We don't have to choose between caring about people's eternal souls and their present physical needs. Both matter because God's redemptive plan encompasses both.

Redemption is both personal and cosmic.

The great exchange we've been exploring doesn't just change individual hearts—it begins the transformation of entire cultures and systems. When people experience God's grace, they naturally work to extend that grace into their communities and institutions.

This perspective also helps us engage constructively with culture rather than retreating from it. We can appreciate what's good while working to redeem what's broken, knowing that our efforts participate in God's ultimate plan.

The cross reveals God's intention to restore everything he originally created good. That includes you, your relationships, your work, and the world itself.

Chapter 7 Toolbox: The Ultimate Swap

- **Atonement**: This is the comprehensive medicine Jesus provided for our souls. It is how His work on the cross fixes our guilt and heals our shame so we can flourish again.
- **Substitution**: This is the beautiful exchange where Jesus takes our sin and our punishment on Himself. In return, He gives us His own peace and His perfect record with God.
- **Christus Victor**: This is the model where Jesus is the hero who wins a war. By dying and rising again, He broke the power of sin and death to set us free from the fears that used to trap us.
- **Cosmic Redemption**: Jesus did not just die to save individual people. He died to start a massive project that will eventually fix and restore everything in the entire universe.

8

RESURRECTION: THE ULTIMATE
GAME CHANGER

Beyond Heaven's Gates Lies Something Greater

I magine telling your friends that Christianity is just about "being good so you can go to heaven when you die." Julian tried this approach when his classmates asked him about his faith, but he quickly realized something was missing. His explanation made Christianity sound like a cosmic reward program – be nice, follow rules, get your ticket to the clouds. But when he discovered what resurrection actually means, everything changed. He wasn't just talking about an escape plan from earth; he was talking about God's ultimate plan to restore and renew everything.

The resurrection isn't God's exit strategy from the physical world – it's His renovation plan for it. Many people, including Christians, misunderstand the ultimate goal of faith as simply "going to heaven." But the biblical picture is far more comprehensive and exciting. God isn't planning to scrap the physical universe and start over with something completely spiritual. Instead, He's planning to resurrect and restore everything, creating "new heavens and a new earth" where the physical and spiritual merge perfectly.

Consider what this means for everything we experience now:

- Physical bodies matter eternally – We won't become ghosts or spirits, but receive perfected physical bodies
- Relationships continue and deepen – The connections we build here have eternal significance
- Creative work has lasting value – Art, music, literature, and innovation contribute to God's renewed world
- Nature itself gets restored – Environmental care becomes an act of faith in God's restoration plan

Margaret always felt guilty about enjoying "worldly" things like art, music, and nature, thinking they distracted from "spiritual" matters. But when she learned that resurrection means God values the physical world enough to renew it rather than destroy it, she realized her love for creativity and beauty actually reflected God's heart. She began to see her artistic talents not as distractions from faith, but as glimpses of the restored world to come. This understanding gave her confidence to discuss with her skeptical art teacher how faith actually enhances rather than diminishes appreciation for physical beauty and creativity.

This connects directly to the great exchange we explored in the previous chapter. Jesus didn't just take our sins and give us His right-eousness so we could escape this world. He made that exchange so we could be part of restoring this world to what God always intended it to be. Our sins separated us from God's restoration project, but through Jesus, we become partners in renewal rather than refugees waiting for evacuation.

The resurrection changes how we approach everything. When you know that your physical body, your relationships, your creative work, and even your care for the environment have eternal significance, ordinary life becomes sacred. Every act of love, every moment of beauty, every effort toward justice becomes a preview of the restored world God is creating.

This also means death isn't the final word.

Death becomes a temporary interruption, not a permanent ending. The people we love, the work we do, the world we inhabit – all of it finds ultimate meaning in God's resurrection plan. This transforms grief from hopeless sorrow into hopeful longing. It changes how we treat our bodies, our relationships, and our planet.

But here's where the story gets even more interesting. God doesn't just promise this restoration for some distant future. He begins the restoration work now, and He invites us to participate. The same Spirit who raised Jesus from the dead works in us today, giving us tastes of that future reality. We experience hints of the restored world through answered prayers, healed relationships, moments of transcendent beauty, and acts of sacrificial love.

This sets the stage for understanding how God's Spirit works in the world today – not as an escape from physical reality, but as the power that begins transforming it from the inside out.

When History Meets Belief

When Isaac got into a heated discussion with his history teacher about whether the resurrection actually happened, he realized he needed more than just "because the Bible says so" as his defense. The teacher challenged him: "Show me real historical evidence that doesn't depend on religious belief." At first, Isaac felt overwhelmed, but as he researched the historical case for resurrection, he discovered that the evidence was stronger than he'd ever imagined – and it didn't require circular reasoning or blind faith.

The resurrection of Jesus isn't just a nice story or spiritual metaphor – it's presented in Scripture as a historical event that happened in real time and space. This matters enormously because Christianity rises or falls on historical claims, not just philosophical ideas. If Jesus didn't actually rise from the dead, then Christianity is false, regardless of how inspiring its teachings might be. But if He did rise from the dead, then everything changes about reality itself.

Consider the historical evidence that even skeptical scholars generally accept:

- Jesus died by crucifixion – This is virtually undisputed among historians, including non-Christian ones
- His tomb was found empty – Multiple independent sources report this, including those initially skeptical
- His followers genuinely believed they encountered Him alive – Their dramatic transformation from fearful deserters to bold martyrs requires explanation
- The movement began in Jerusalem – Christianity started in the very city where Jesus was killed, where contrary evidence would be easiest to produce

Emily felt intimidated when her college-bound cousin challenged her faith as "wishful thinking with no real evidence." But she had been studying the historical case for resurrection and calmly presented three facts that even skeptical historians generally accept: Jesus died by crucifixion, His tomb was found empty, and His followers genuinely believed they saw Him alive again. She explained that while people can debate the interpretation of these facts, the facts themselves are historically solid. Her cousin was surprised by the strength of the evidence and admitted he had never seriously considered the historical case. This conversation gave Emily confidence that her faith could engage honestly with academic scrutiny.

This historical foundation connects powerfully to the great exchange we explored earlier. The exchange of our sin for Jesus's righteousness isn't just a theological concept – it's anchored in a historical event. When Jesus died on the cross, that was history. When He rose from the dead, that was history too. The spiritual reality of our reconciliation with God flows from these historical facts.

The historical nature of resurrection also explains why it's such a game changer. If resurrection were just a nice idea or spiritual symbol, it might inspire us but wouldn't fundamentally alter reality. But if it actually happened – if death itself was conquered in space and time – then the rules of existence have permanently changed.

This is where the evidence becomes particularly compelling. The disciples' transformation from scared, scattered followers into bold proclamators of resurrection requires explanation. People don't typically suffer persecution and death for what they know to be a lie. Yet these same disciples who abandoned Jesus during His arrest later faced imprisonment, torture, and execution rather than deny His resurrection.

The rapid spread of Christianity in Jerusalem also demands explanation. This was the worst possible place to start a movement based on false claims about Jesus. The authorities who killed Him were right there. The tomb was right there. If the body was still in the ground, producing it would have crushed Christianity immediately.

But none of these counter-evidences appeared.

Instead, within weeks of the crucifixion, thousands in Jerusalem were converting to Christianity. Something extraordinary had clearly happened.

This historical foundation sets us up to understand how the same power that raised Jesus from the dead continues working in the world today through God's Spirit – not as mystical wishful thinking, but as historical reality extending into our present experience.

Living Backwards from Forever

Nathan used to think that believing in resurrection was mainly about what happens after death – something for the distant future that didn't affect his daily choices. But during his grandmother's battle with cancer, everything shifted. As he watched her face her illness with incredible peace and even joy, she explained that resurrection hope wasn't just about "someday" – it was transforming how she lived today. She wasn't just enduring suffering; she was seeing it as temporary in light of the permanent restoration coming. Her hope wasn't passive waiting but active living with unshakeable confidence in God's ultimate victory.

Resurrection hope radically transforms how Christians approach present challenges, relationships, and decisions. It's not pie-in-the-sky thinking that ignores current problems, but rather a foundation that provides perspective and strength for engaging current problems. When you truly believe that God will ultimately restore everything broken, you can face temporary setbacks with resilience, invest in relationships knowing they have eternal significance, and work for justice knowing that righteousness will ultimately triumph.

This hope changes everything about how we live now:

- Suffering becomes bearable when viewed as temporary rather than ultimate
- Relationships gain deeper meaning when seen in light of eternal restoration
- Work and creativity become participation in God's ongoing renewal of the world
- Justice efforts gain motivation from confidence in ultimate victory over evil
- Death loses its terror because it becomes a transition, not an ending

Rebecca struggled with anxiety about climate change and social injustice, feeling overwhelmed by problems too big for her to solve. But when she grasped resurrection hope, her perspective shifted dramatically. She realized that her environmental efforts and social justice work weren't desperate attempts to save a doomed world, but participation in God's restoration project. This hope didn't make her passive – instead, it energized her activism with confidence that her efforts aligned with God's ultimate plan. When friends asked how she maintained such optimism while staying realistic about serious problems, she could explain how resurrection hope provides both honest assessment of current brokenness and unshakeable confidence in ultimate restoration.

This connects directly to the great exchange we explored earlier. Because Jesus took our condemnation and gave us His righteousness, we're not just forgiven – we're invited into His restoration project. We become partners with God in bringing glimpses of the restored world into our current reality. Every act of love, justice, creativity, and healing becomes a preview of the resurrection life to come.

Living with resurrection hope means making decisions based on ultimate reality rather than immediate appearances. When a friendship hits rough patches, you invest in reconciliation because relationships have eternal significance. When facing career choices, you consider not just financial success but how your work contributes to human flourishing. When encountering suffering, you respond with compassion because you know pain isn't the final word.

This hope also transforms how we handle failure and disappointment. When projects fail, relationships end, or dreams get crushed, resurrection hope reminds us that God specializes in bringing life from death. Our current setbacks don't define our ultimate future. This doesn't mean we ignore pain or pretend everything is fine, but it means we grieve with hope rather than despair.

Perhaps most importantly, resurrection hope changes how we view other people. Everyone around us – family enemies, strangers – has eternal significance. The person who annoys you in class, the teacher who seems impossible, the sibling who drives you crazy – all of them are candidates for God's restoration project. This transforms how we treat people, knowing that our interactions have consequences that extend far beyond this life.

This foundation of hope sets us up to understand how God's Spirit works in the present, bringing resurrection power into our daily experience and relationships.

Death Defeated, Promise Fulfilled

When Marcus attended his great-uncle's funeral, he heard the pastor say that Jesus' resurrection was the "firstfruits" of resurrection for all believers. At first, this sounded like nice religious language that didn't mean much practically. But as Marcus thought about it more, he realized this connection was actually the key to understanding both death and life. Jesus' resurrection wasn't just a unique miracle that proved His divinity – it was the preview and guarantee of what awaits everyone who trusts in Him.

Jesus' resurrection serves as both the prototype and the promise of future resurrection for all believers. The term "firstfruits" indicates that Jesus' resurrection was the first installment of a larger harvest to come.

This means that what happened to Jesus' body – not just spiritual survival but physical transformation and renewal – will happen to everyone who belongs to Him. His resurrection demonstrates what our resurrection bodies will be like: real and physical, but transformed and perfected.

The Gospel accounts provide fascinating details about Jesus' resurrection body that hint at our future:

- Recognizable yet transformed – His disciples knew it was Him, suggesting continuity with our current bodies
- Physical but enhanced – He could eat food and be touched, proving genuine physical existence
- Powerful beyond current limitations – He appeared through walls and traveled instantly, showing enhanced capabilities
- Perfect and incorruptible – No longer subject to decay, aging, or death

Sarah always wondered what would happen to her grandmother who died with Alzheimer's disease, or her cousin who was born with severe physical disabilities. The idea of just "souls going to heaven" seemed to suggest their physical struggles were ultimately meaningless. But when she understood that Jesus' resurrection promises transformed physical bodies, everything clicked. Her grandmother would be resurrected with a perfected mind, her cousin with a perfected body. Their current limitations weren't permanent features but temporary conditions that resurrection would completely heal. This understanding helped her explain to doubting friends why Christianity offers genuine hope for people facing physical and mental challenges, not just spiritual comfort.

This promise connects powerfully to the great exchange we explored earlier. Through Jesus' death and resurrection, we don't just receive forgiveness for our sins – we receive His resurrection life. The same power that raised Jesus from the dead becomes available to us, both for transformation in this life and for ultimate resurrection in the future. This exchange means that death has lost its ultimate victory over those who belong to Christ.

The resurrection promise also addresses one of humanity's deepest fears: the fear that death makes everything meaningless. If consciousness simply ends at death, then all our relationships, achievements, and experiences become ultimately pointless. But resurrection promise says that everything valuable about human existence gets preserved, restored, and perfected. The love you share, the beauty you create, the relationships you build – all of it has eternal significance because you will be raised to experience it in perfected form.

This hope transforms grief from hopeless sorrow into hope-filled longing.

When believers face the death of loved ones, they don't grieve as those who have no hope. They grieve because separation is real and painful, but they grieve with confidence that the separation is temporary. The resurrection promise means that saying goodbye is not forever, but "see you later."

Understanding resurrection as God's ultimate victory over death also provides courage for facing our own mortality. Death becomes not a terrifying unknown, but a doorway to complete restoration. This doesn't eliminate the natural human fear of dying, but it does provide hope that transcends that fear.

This resurrection hope sets the stage for understanding how God's Spirit works in believers today – bringing the power of resurrection life into our current experience while we wait for its complete fulfillment.

Chapter 8 Toolbox: Life 2.0

- **First fruits**: This describes Jesus coming back to life as the first sample of a much larger harvest. It is the prototype that proves our future bodies will be real and physical but also transformed and perfected.
- **New Creation**: God is not planning to throw the earth in the trash and move us to a cloud. He is going to renovate and restore everything to create new heavens and a new earth where the physical and spiritual worlds merge perfectly.
- **Incorruptible**: This describes our future resurrection bodies

that will never again be subject to things like decay, aging, or death.

- **Resurrection Hope**: This is more than just a nice thought for the future. It is the foundation that gives us the strength to face challenges, invest in relationships, and work for justice today because we know God will ultimately win .

THE SPIRIT'S QUIET REVOLUTION

The Holy Spirit's Personal Touch

Harrison always thought of the Holy Spirit like electricity—a powerful force that could turn on the lights of faith when he needed it most. But during a youth group discussion about prayer, his pastor asked, "Do you talk to electricity, or do you flip a switch?" That simple question revolutionized how Harrison understood the third person of the Trinity. The Holy Spirit isn't an impersonal energy we tap into; He's a divine person who thinks, feels, and acts with intention and love.

The Holy Spirit possesses all the attributes of personhood that distinguish Him from mere spiritual energy or divine influence. He demonstrates intellect by teaching and revealing truth, emotions by being grieved when we sin, and will by directing the early church's missionary efforts. Understanding this personal dimension transforms how we relate to God's Spirit—from trying to manipulate a force to developing a relationship with a person.

Evidence of the Spirit's Personhood:

- The Spirit has intellect: He teaches, reminds, and reveals truth to believers (John 14:26)
- The Spirit has emotions: He can be grieved by our sin and pleased by our obedience (Ephesians 4:30)
- The Spirit has will: He distributes spiritual gifts as He chooses and directs ministry decisions (1 Corinthians 12:11, Acts 16:6-7)

Elizabeth struggled with feeling distant from God until she realized she had been treating the Holy Spirit like a spiritual vending machine —putting in good behavior and expecting blessings to come out. When her mentor explained that the Spirit was actually grieving over her transactional approach to faith, Elizabeth began apologizing to the Holy Spirit directly and asking Him what He wanted for her life. This shift from manipulation to relationship opened up a completely new dimension of spiritual intimacy she never knew was possible.

The resurrection we explored in the previous chapter makes the Spirit's personal presence possible in our lives today. Jesus promised that after His resurrection and ascension, He would send another Helper who would be with us forever. This Helper wouldn't just visit occasionally or show up during emergencies—He would take up permanent residence in every believer's heart.

The Spirit's personal involvement in our lives happens through several key ways that demonstrate His caring nature and intentional work:

How the Spirit Shows His Personal Care:

- Conviction: He gently points out sin not to condemn but to restore relationship
- Comfort: He provides peace during difficult circumstances and emotional pain
- Guidance: He helps us make decisions that align with God's will and character
- Intercession: He prays for us when we don't know what to say (Romans 8:26)

Harrison discovered this during his parents' divorce when he found himself unable to pray coherently. His youth pastor explained that the

Holy Spirit was interceding for him with groans too deep for words, translating his broken heart into perfect prayers that reached God's throne. This knowledge transformed Harrison's understanding of prayer from a performance to a conversation where the Spirit actively participated.

The Spirit's personal touch also appears in His role as our internal teacher and guide. Unlike external authorities who give rules from a distance, the Holy Spirit works from within our hearts to help us understand Scripture, recognize God's voice, and develop spiritual wisdom. He doesn't override our personalities or force decisions upon us, but rather works through our thoughts, emotions, and circumstances to lead us toward God's best plans.

This personal relationship with the Holy Spirit prepares us for the transformation we'll explore next—how His quiet revolution within us helps us become fully human again. The Spirit doesn't just comfort or guide us; He actively works to restore the image of God that sin damaged, making us more like Jesus from the inside out.

The Spirit's Journey Through Hearts and Calling

The Holy Spirit operates like a master craftsman working on three simultaneous projects in every believer's life. In conversion, He's the architect drawing up the blueprints for new life. In sanctification, He's the contractor doing the daily renovation work. In mission, He's the project manager coordinating how our transformed lives fit into God's larger construction project of building His kingdom. Each role is distinct but interconnected, creating a comprehensive work that spans from our initial salvation to our final glorification.

The Spirit's work follows a divine progression that begins before we even recognize our need for God and continues throughout our earthly lives and beyond. This comprehensive ministry ensures that salvation is not just a one-time event but an ongoing transformation that equips us for eternal purpose.

The Spirit's Three-Fold Ministry:

- Conversion work: Convicts of sin, reveals Christ's truth, and regenerates the human heart (John 16:8-11)
- Sanctification work: Produces spiritual fruit, breaks strongholds, and conforms us to Christ's image (Galatians 5:22-23)
- Mission work: Empowers witness, opens doors for ministry, and coordinates the global spread of the gospel (Acts 1:8)

Bradley couldn't understand why he felt compelled to share his faith with his skeptical lab partner in chemistry class until he learned about the Spirit's role in mission. Every time Bradley felt that gentle nudge to ask his partner about spiritual things, he was experiencing the same Spirit who had directed Philip to the Ethiopian eunuch and Paul to Macedonia. Recognizing this pattern helped Bradley trust those promptings and eventually led to his lab partner asking serious questions about Christianity. The Spirit had been orchestrating divine appointments that Bradley had almost dismissed as coincidence.

The conversion work of the Spirit demonstrates His personal involvement in bringing people to faith. He doesn't force decisions but creates the conditions where people can genuinely choose Christ. This includes opening blind spiritual eyes to see the beauty of the gospel, softening hard hearts to receive God's love, and providing the faith necessary to trust in Jesus' finished work. Without the Spirit's regenerating power, the resurrection we discussed in the previous chapter would remain merely historical fact rather than personal reality.

Laura experienced this when she attended her friend's baptism service. As the pastor explained the gospel, she felt an overwhelming sense of her own need for forgiveness and simultaneously a deep assurance that Jesus had already provided it. She described it as scales falling from her eyes—suddenly the Bible verses her Christian friends had quoted made perfect sense, and she understood why they seemed so passionate about their faith. The Spirit had been preparing her heart for months through circumstances and conversations she hadn't recognized as divine appointments.

Sanctification represents the Spirit's ongoing work to make us more like Christ in our thoughts, attitudes, and actions. This process connects directly to the resurrection power we explored earlier, as the same Spirit who raised Jesus from the dead now lives within believers to produce spiritual transformation. The Spirit produces fruit in our character—love, joy, peace, patience, kindness, goodness, faithfulness, gentleness, and self-control—not through human effort but through divine empowerment.

The Spirit's mission work extends beyond individual transformation to global kingdom purposes. He coordinates the church's witness by opening doors for ministry, providing boldness to share the gospel, and preparing hearts to receive the message. This work connects every believer to the larger story of God's redemptive plan, making our personal sanctification part of a worldwide movement.

These three dimensions of the Spirit's work prepare us for what we'll explore next—how His transforming power helps us become fully human again. The Spirit doesn't just save us from something; He saves us for something. His quiet revolution within our hearts restores the image of God that sin damaged, preparing us to live as the new creation God always intended us to be.

Divine Powers Meet Daily Purpose

When Sophia discovered she had the spiritual gift of encouragement, she initially felt disappointed—she had been hoping for something more dramatic like prophecy or healing. But her youth pastor helped her understand that spiritual gifts aren't about creating a spiritual hierarchy; they're about empowering ordinary believers to serve in extraordinary ways. Her gift of encouragement had already prevented two friends from making destructive decisions and helped launch a peer counseling ministry at school. What seemed ordinary was actually the Spirit's supernatural work flowing through her natural personality and learned skills.

Spiritual gifts represent the Holy Spirit's distribution of divine abilities to accomplish supernatural purposes through natural means. These gifts aren't spiritual party tricks designed to impress others, but practical tools for building up the church and advancing God's kingdom in everyday contexts.

Understanding Spiritual Gifts:

- Gifts are diverse but unified: Different abilities serve the same purpose of building up the body of Christ (1 Corinthians 12:4-7)
- Gifts are supernatural but practical: Divine empowerment for real-world ministry needs and opportunities (Romans 12:6-8)
- Gifts are individual but communal: Each person receives unique gifts that complement and complete others' gifts (1 Corinthians 12:12-27)

Marcus thought his analytical mind was just a natural talent until he started using it to help younger students understand difficult Bible passages. His gift of teaching became evident when these students began growing in their faith and asking deeper theological questions. The Spirit had taken Marcus's natural intellectual curiosity and supernaturally empowered it for ministry. Now he's considering becoming a youth pastor, realizing that his "ordinary" ability to explain complex concepts is actually an extraordinary gift from the Spirit.

The resurrection power we explored in Chapter 8 directly connects to spiritual gifts—the same Spirit who raised Jesus from the dead now works through believers to accomplish supernatural ministry. This isn't about human talent enhanced by divine blessing, but about the Spirit using human vessels to display God's power in practical ways. Every spiritual gift reflects some aspect of Christ's ministry, making believers living extensions of His ongoing work in the world.

Spiritual gifts often operate through what appears to be natural ability, but the results exceed what human skill alone could accomplish. Rachel discovered this when her natural compassion for hurting people began producing unusual results—people consistently opened up to her about deep struggles, found healing through her prayers, and experienced peace in her presence that they couldn't explain. Her gift of mercy wasn't just emotional sensitivity; it was the Spirit using her natural empathy to channel divine comfort to broken hearts.

The diversity of spiritual gifts reflects the Trinity's creative nature and ensures that every believer has something unique to contribute. No gift is more important than others, just as no part of the human body is unnecessary. This prevents spiritual pride and promotes genuine community where everyone's contribution matters.

Common Categories of Spiritual Gifts:

- Speaking gifts: Teaching, prophecy, encouragement, evangelism
- Serving gifts: Helps, administration, giving, hospitality
- Supernatural gifts: Healing, miracles, discernment, tongues

Discovering and developing spiritual gifts requires both personal reflection and community input. The gifts often emerge naturally as believers serve others and respond to needs around them. What energizes you? Where do you see unusual results? What do other believers consistently affirm in your ministry?

The Spirit's gift distribution prepares believers for the transformation we'll explore next—becoming fully human again. These gifts aren't just tools for ministry; they're expressions of who God created us to be. As the Spirit works through our unique gifts, we discover our true identity and calling, experiencing the joy of functioning as God originally designed. The quiet revolution continues as supernatural power meets daily purpose, transforming ordinary people into extraordinary instruments of divine grace.

When God Moves vs When We Feel

The challenge of discerning between genuine spiritual experiences and emotional manipulation became real for Amanda during a youth conference where the speaker seemed to be manufacturing spiritual moments through dramatic music and emotional appeals. She felt confused when she didn't experience the same intense feelings as her friends, wondering if something was wrong with her faith. Later, her mentor helped her understand that the Spirit's work is characterized by truth, peace, and alignment with Scripture—not necessarily by emotional intensity or crowd dynamics.

Learning to distinguish between the Spirit's authentic work and human emotion or manipulation is crucial for developing mature faith that can withstand real-world challenges. This discernment protects believers from both spiritual deception and emotional burnout while helping them recognize genuine divine activity.

Tests for Authentic Spiritual Experience:

- The Spirit's work aligns with Scripture: Authentic spiritual experiences will never contradict biblical truth (1 John 4:1-3)
- The Spirit's work produces lasting fruit: Genuine spiritual activity results in long-term character change, not just temporary emotional highs (Galatians 5:22-23)
- The Spirit's work brings peace and clarity: Divine guidance typically comes with a sense of peace and growing understanding, not confusion or pressure (1 Corinthians 14:33)

Tyler learned this lesson when he felt "led by the Spirit" to ask out a girl who was already in a committed relationship. His youth pastor helped him realize that the Spirit would never lead him to pursue something that could damage others' relationships or compromise biblical principles. What Tyler had interpreted as spiritual guidance was actually his own desire dressed up in spiritual language. This experience taught him to test his impressions against Scripture and seek wise counsel before attributing his impulses to the Holy Spirit.

Emotional experiences aren't necessarily unspiritual, but they require careful evaluation. The Spirit often works through our emotions, bringing conviction that produces godly sorrow or joy that reflects divine blessing. However, emotions can also be manufactured through music, peer pressure, or skilled speakers who know how to manipulate crowd psychology. The key difference lies in the source and the fruit—authentic spiritual emotion springs from truth and produces lasting transformation.

Warning Signs of Manipulation:

- High-pressure tactics demanding immediate emotional response

- Claims that questioning the experience shows lack of faith
- Emphasis on feelings over biblical truth
- Results that don't align with Scripture or produce lasting change

Sarah experienced this when a visiting speaker pressured students to make dramatic public commitments during an emotionally charged altar call. She felt uncomfortable with the manipulation but worried she was being unspiritual. Later reflection revealed that genuine conviction comes with peace about the decision, time to count the cost, and alignment with God's revealed will in Scripture.

The resurrection power we discussed earlier provides the foundation for authentic spiritual experience. The same Spirit who raised Jesus works in believers to produce real transformation, not manufactured emotion. This power operates through truth, not hype, creating lasting change rather than temporary spiritual highs.

Developing spiritual discernment requires growing in biblical knowledge, seeking wise counsel, and paying attention to long-term fruit rather than immediate feelings. The Spirit's work typically brings increasing freedom, joy, and Christ-likeness over time, while manipulation produces dependence on external emotional stimulation.

Practical Steps for Discernment:

- Test experiences against Scripture
- Seek counsel from mature believers
- Look for lasting fruit and character change
- Notice whether the experience brings freedom or bondage

The Spirit's quiet revolution in our hearts prepares us for genuine transformation—not just emotional experiences, but actual change that makes us more like Christ. This authentic work sets the stage for what we'll explore next: how the Spirit's transforming power helps us become fully human again, restoring the image of God that sin damaged and enabling us to live as the new creation God always intended us to be.

Chapter 9 Toolbox: The Helper Within

- **The Spirit is a Person**: The Holy Spirit isn't just a vibe or some spiritual energy like electricity. He is a real person who thinks, feels, and acts with intentional love toward you .
- **Regeneration**: This is the Spirit's conversion work where He brings your soul to life. He opens your eyes to see how beautiful the gospel is and gives you the faith to trust Jesus.
- **Sanctification**: Think of this as the Spirit's daily renovation project in your life. He slowly reshapes your character to look more like Jesus by producing fruit like love, joy, and patience.
- **Spiritual Gifts**: These are special abilities the Spirit gives you to help others and build up the church . They aren't spiritual party tricks but tools that help your natural personality accomplish extraordinary things .

10

BECOMING HUMAN AGAIN

Salvation Rebuilds What Sin Destroyed

John had always thought of salvation like getting a "Get Out of Jail Free" card - a cosmic pardon that kept him from going to hell. But when his youth pastor asked him what he was saved for, not just what he was saved from, John realized he'd been missing half the picture. Salvation wasn't just about escaping punishment; it was about becoming fully human again, the way God originally designed us to be.

Remember back in Chapter 5 when we explored how sin fractured everything? but when you arrived, you found it had been vandalized and left in ruins. The windows were shattered, the walls were covered in graffiti, and the foundation had cracks running through it. You could choose to just camp out in one corner and ignore the damage, or you could begin the long process of restoration. Salvation is God saying, "I'm going to help you restore this place to its original beauty."

Brief Explanation

Salvation encompasses both justification - being declared righteous before God - and the ongoing process of restoration to our original design as image-bearers of God. It's not merely about avoiding hell, but about experiencing abundant life now and eternally. When Jesus talked about coming to give us life "to the full," he wasn't just talking about heaven someday. He was talking about becoming the people we were always meant to be.

We're Restored to Relationship with God

Sin broke our connection to our Creator, but salvation rebuilds that bridge, allowing us to know God personally and intimately. Before salvation, trying to connect with God was like attempting to call someone when your phone has no signal - lots of frustration and static, but no real communication. Salvation doesn't just give you signal bars; it gives you a direct line to the Creator of the universe.

This restoration means prayer becomes actual conversation instead of wishful thinking. Reading the Bible transforms from homework into hearing from someone who loves you. And that nagging sense that something is missing from your life? It starts to fade as you discover the relationship you were designed for.

We're Restored to Our True Purpose

Instead of living for temporary pleasures or achievements, we redis-cover our calling to reflect God's character and participate in His mission. This doesn't mean everyone becomes a missionary or pastor. It means the accountant starts seeing their work as serving others with excellence. The athlete realizes their platform can encourage team-mates. The artist discovers their creativity reflects God's own creative nature.

Your true purpose isn't about finding your dream job or becoming famous.

It's about becoming someone who shows the world what God is like.

We're Restored to Authentic Community

Salvation heals our broken relationships with others, enabling us to love sacrificially and build genuine connections. Sin made us self-centered, competitive, and afraid of vulnerability. But as God's Spirit works in us, we start caring more about others' success than our own image. We become people others can trust with their struggles because we've experienced grace ourselves.

Case Study

Ava struggled with perfectionism and anxiety throughout high school. She thought becoming a Christian meant adding more rules to follow perfectly. But when her small group leader explained that salvation meant God was restoring her to who she was meant to be - free from the pressure to earn love through performance - everything changed.

She began to see her worth as rooted in God's love, not her achievements. Her anxiety decreased as she learned to rest in her identity as God's beloved daughter, and she found herself naturally wanting to serve others out of gratitude rather than obligation.

This restoration process takes time, but it's already begun. As we'll see in the next chapter, part of this rebuilding happens within the community of believers - the family that chooses you even as you choose them.

When Transformation Takes Root

Ryan became a Christian at summer camp with tears streaming down his face, expecting to wake up the next morning as a completely different person. When he still struggled with anger and selfishness, he wondered if his conversion was even real. His mentor explained that becoming like Jesus is a lifelong journey called sanctification - and it's actually more encouraging than instant transformation would be.

Think of it like learning to play guitar. You don't become a virtuoso overnight, even if you have natural talent. Your fingers need to develop calluses, your muscle memory needs time to form, and your ear needs training to recognize when something sounds right. But every day of practice makes you better than you were before.

Sanctification works the same way.

Brief Explanation

Sanctification is the gradual process by which the Holy Spirit transforms believers to become more like Christ. It involves both God's supernatural work and our active participation, happening over time through various means of grace. Remember from Chapter 9 how the Spirit works quietly in our lives? This is one of His primary jobs - slowly reshaping our hearts, minds, and habits to reflect Jesus' character.

The word "sanctification" simply means "being made holy" or "set apart for God's purposes." It's what happens after justification, when God declares us righteous. While justification is instant and complete, sanctification is ongoing and gradual. It starts the moment you become a Christian and continues until you meet Jesus face to face.

It's a Partnership Between God and Us

The Holy Spirit provides the power for change, but we must cooperate by making choices that align with God's will and putting ourselves in positions where growth can happen. This isn't about earning your salvation - that's already settled through Christ's work on the cross. Instead, it's about working together with God as He transforms you from the inside out.

God won't force change on you like some cosmic puppet master. He invites you to participate in your own transformation. When you feel the Spirit prompting you to forgive someone who hurt you, you can choose to obey or resist. When you're tempted to lie to avoid consequences, you can choose honesty or deception. These daily choices matter because they either cooperate with or resist the Spirit's work in your life.

It Happens Through Ordinary Means

God typically uses regular spiritual practices like Bible reading, prayer, worship, and community rather than dramatic supernatural interventions. This might seem disappointing if you're hoping for a lightning-bolt moment that instantly fixes all your problems. But God's normal way of changing people is through consistent, ordinary activities done with faith and expectation.

Reading the Bible renews your mind by showing you God's perspective on life. Prayer connects you to the power source you need for lasting change. Worship reminds you of God's greatness and your identity in Him. Christian community provides encouragement, accountability, and examples of what spiritual maturity looks like.

Progress Isn't Always Linear

Growth often involves setbacks, struggles, and seasons of seeming stagnation, but God is faithful to complete the work He started. Some weeks you'll feel like you're making huge strides in patience or self-control. Other weeks you'll wonder if you've made any progress at all. This is completely normal and doesn't mean God has given up on you.

Case Study

Madison had a terrible relationship with her younger brother, constantly fighting and saying hurtful things. After becoming a Christian, she expected to automatically become patient and kind, but found herself still losing her temper. Her discipleship group helped her understand that change happens through practice - choosing forgiveness when she didn't feel like it, praying for her brother when he annoyed her, and asking the Holy Spirit for self-control in heated moments.

Over months, she noticed her heart genuinely softening toward him. The change was real, but it came through faithful choices over time, not a single moment of transformation. This process of growing together with other believers points us toward the next part of our journey - discovering how the family of God shapes who we become.

Forged Through Fellowship and Fire

When Marcus first heard about "spiritual disciplines," he pictured medieval monks in isolated monasteries, whipping themselves for spiritual points. But his youth pastor painted a different picture: spiritual disciplines are like training routines for athletes, and the Christian community is like a team that trains together. Even suffering, as unwelcome as it is, can serve as an unexpected coach in developing spiritual strength.

Remember from Chapter 9 how the Spirit works quietly in our lives? He often uses three main tools to shape us into people who look more like Jesus. Think of them as God's construction crew for the ongoing renovation project that is your life. Each tool serves a different purpose, but they work together to build something beautiful.

Brief Explanation

God uses three primary means to shape us into Christ's likeness: Christian community for encouragement and accountability, spiritual disciplines for intentional growth practices, and suffering to develop perseverance and dependence on Him. This might sound like a strange combination - fellowship, personal practices, and hardship - but each plays a crucial role in spiritual formation.

This process builds on everything we've learned so far. The Trinity provides the relational model for community. The Bible guides our understanding of spiritual practices. Christ's work on the cross gives meaning to our suffering. And the Spirit empowers it all.

Community Provides Accountability and Encouragement

Other believers help us see our blind spots, celebrate our growth, and support us through difficult seasons in ways we couldn't manage alone. You can't see the back of your own head without a mirror, and you can't see your spiritual blind spots without other people who love you enough to speak truth.

Christian community isn't just about having friends who share your beliefs. It's about being known deeply enough that people can call out both your strengths and your weaknesses. When you're struggling with pride, a good friend will lovingly point it out. When you're growing in generosity, they'll celebrate that progress with you.

This is why isolated Christianity doesn't work well.

You need other believers in your life who are further along the path than you are, people who are walking alongside you, and newer believers you can encourage and mentor.

Spiritual Disciplines Create Space for God to Work

Practices like prayer, Bible study, fasting, and service position our hearts to receive from God and respond in obedience. These aren't magic rituals that automatically make you more spiritual. Instead, they're like clearing weeds from a garden so good seeds can grow.

Prayer opens your heart to hear God's voice throughout your day. Regular Bible reading renews your mind with God's perspective. Fasting breaks the power of physical appetites and creates hunger for spiritual things. Serving others gets your focus off yourself and onto God's mission in the world.

The key is consistency over intensity. Reading your Bible for ten minutes every day for a year will transform you more than reading it for three hours once a month.

Suffering Develops Character and Dependence

While God doesn't cause all suffering, He uses difficult circumstances to build our faith, deepen our compassion, and teach us to rely on His strength rather than our own. This is probably the hardest part to understand and accept. Nobody signs up for pain and hardship, but they often become the most powerful tools God uses to shape our character.

Suffering strips away our illusions of control and self-sufficiency. It teaches us to depend on God's strength when our own runs out. It also gives us genuine compassion for others who are hurting.

Case Study

Sarah was devastated when her parents divorced during her junior year. She felt angry at God and questioned whether He really cared about her family. Her small group didn't try to fix her pain with easy answers, but they consistently showed up - bringing meals, listening to her vent, and praying with her when she couldn't find words.

During this season, she also discovered that journaling her prayers helped her process her emotions honestly before God. Looking back a year later, she could see how the combination of community support, honest communication with God, and walking through the pain rather than avoiding it had developed a deeper, more resilient faith than she'd had before the crisis.

This process of growing together points us toward something bigger - the family of believers that becomes home.

Dancing on the Edge of Eternity

Derek felt confused when his pastor talked about being "new creations" while also acknowledging that Christians still sin and struggle. Was he transformed or wasn't he? His confusion cleared when someone explained the "already/not yet" reality: we're already forgiven and adopted as God's children, but we're not yet fully like Jesus and won't be until heaven. This tension explains both the hope and the struggle of Christian life.

Picture being accepted to your dream college but still having to finish your senior year of high school. You're already a college student in some ways - you have your acceptance letter, you can wear the school's sweatshirt, and you know where you're headed. But you're not yet living the full college experience. You still have homework, curfews, and cafeteria food to endure.

This is what theologians call the "already/not yet" tension.

Brief Explanation

Christians live in the tension between what God has already accomplished through Christ - forgiveness, adoption, new nature - and what He will complete in the future: perfect holiness, resurrection bodies, no more sin or suffering. Understanding this tension helps explain why believers experience both victory and struggle.

When the Spirit began His quiet revolution in your life, as we explored in Chapter 9, He didn't remove you from this world or instantly perfect you. Instead, He began a transformation process that won't be completed until Christ returns or calls you home to heaven.

We Have a New Nature But Still Battle the Old

The Holy Spirit has given us new desires and capabilities, but our old sinful patterns haven't disappeared and won't until we're glorified in heaven. This explains why you can genuinely love Jesus and still struggle with anger, pride, or selfishness. It's not that your conversion wasn't real; it's that the transformation isn't yet complete.

Think of it like renovating an old house while you're still living in it. The new kitchen is beautiful and functional, but the upstairs bathroom still has peeling wallpaper and a leaky faucet. Both realities exist simultaneously until the renovation is finished.

Your new nature creates desires to please God, serve others, and grow in holiness. But your old patterns of thinking and behaving haven't been completely erased yet. This creates an internal conflict that every Christian experiences.

We're Citizens of Heaven Living on Earth

Our ultimate allegiance is to God's kingdom, but we must navigate life in a fallen world with different values and systems. This creates practical challenges as we try to live according to biblical principles in contexts that often oppose or ignore those principles.

You might find yourself being the only person in your friend group who chooses not to participate in gossip. Or you might struggle with how to respond to injustice in ways that reflect both truth and grace. These tensions aren't signs of spiritual failure; they're the natural result of representing heaven's values on earth.

Perseverance is Possible Because of God's Faithfulness

True believers may struggle and even fall into serious sin, but God's commitment to complete His work in us means genuine faith will endure to the end. This doesn't mean Christians never doubt or fail significantly. It means that God's grip on us is stronger than our grip on Him.

When you mess up badly, the question isn't whether you've lost your salvation. The question is whether you'll allow that failure to drive you toward God or away from Him.

Case Study

Emma had been a Christian for three years when she fell into a pattern of lying to her parents about where she was going and what she was doing. She felt terrible guilt and wondered if she had lost her salvation or if she had ever really been saved at all.

Her youth leader helped her understand that while her sin was serious and needed to be addressed, it didn't negate her relationship with God. Instead, her very guilt over the sin showed that the Holy Spirit was still at work in her heart. She confessed to her parents, faced the consequences, and put accountability measures in place.

This experience actually strengthened her assurance of salvation as she experienced God's forgiveness and saw His power to help her change, even after serious failure. She learned that the "already/not yet" tension means Christians can expect both spiritual growth and ongoing struggles until we reach our heavenly home.

This reality of living between two worlds leads us naturally to consider how we relate to the family of believers who share this same journey.

Chapter 10 Toolbox: Becoming Who You Are

- **Justification**: This is the legal moment where God declares you are righteous because of what Jesus did instead of how well you performed.
- **Already and Not Yet**: This is the tension of being a new creation who is already forgiven while still living in a world where things are messy and you still struggle with sin .
- **Means of Grace**: These are the daily habits like prayer or reading the Bible that God uses to keep you growing and healthy .
- **Spiritual Disciplines**: These are like a training routine for an athlete where you make space for God to work in your life rather than trying to win points with Him

THE FAMILY YOU CHOOSE AND THE ONE THAT CHOOSES YOU

The Church's Hidden and Seen Faces

When Adam first started attending youth group, he thought church was just the building where his family went on Sundays. But after a mission trip where he saw believers from different denominations working together to serve hurricane victims, his understanding expanded. He realized that the church existed both as the local congregation he could see and touch, and as something much larger—a global, eternal family that transcended buildings and denominations.

The church operates on two levels that seem contradictory but are actually complementary. The visible church includes all the local congregations, denominations, and institutions we can observe and participate in. Think of it as the church you can point to on a map or visit on a Sunday morning. The invisible church encompasses all true believers throughout history and across the globe—a spiritual reality that only God can fully see.

This isn't just theological talk.

Understanding this dual nature helps us navigate the tension between the church's human imperfections and its divine calling. When we grasp both aspects, we can engage meaningfully with our local church while maintaining perspective about the broader work God is doing through his people everywhere.

Key differences between visible and invisible church:

- Visible church includes imperfect people learning to follow Christ together, complete with organizational structures, traditions, and yes, flaws
- Invisible church represents the true spiritual unity of all believers, past and present, regardless of denominational boundaries
- Visible church has membership rolls, budgets, and building committees
- Invisible church transcends human categories and earthly limitations

Both aspects matter deeply. We need the visible church for community, accountability, teaching, and practical Christian living. We gather together because isolation breeds spiritual weakness, and we need the encouragement and correction that comes from doing life alongside other believers. The invisible church, meanwhile, reminds us of our eternal identity and universal connection to something far greater than our local congregation.

Julia struggled with doubt when her church went through a painful split over worship styles. She felt disillusioned watching people she respected argue bitterly about drums versus organs. The building felt heavy with tension every Sunday, and she wondered if this was really what Jesus had in mind when he talked about his followers. Her mentor helped her see that while the visible church can disappoint us with its human messiness, the invisible church—the eternal family of faith—remains unshaken by our temporary conflicts.

This perspective helped Julia find a new church home while maintaining relationships with believers from her former congregation, understanding that they were still part of the same spiritual family despite attending different buildings.

The invisible church connects us to believers we'll never meet on earth. When persecution forces Christians in other countries to worship in secret, they're still part of our spiritual family. When believers from centuries past faced martyrdom for their faith, they walked the same path we walk today. This connection isn't sentimental—it's real and powerful.

Remember how we discussed becoming human again in the previous chapter? The church plays a crucial role in this transformation process. The visible church provides the practical environment where we learn to love difficult people, serve others sacrificially, and practice forgiveness. The invisible church reminds us that this work extends far beyond our immediate circle and connects us to God's eternal purposes.

As we look toward understanding how the future changes everything today, remember that the church exists in both present reality and future hope. We participate in the visible church now while belonging to the invisible church that will one day be revealed in all its glory.

The family you choose meets the family that chooses you.

Finding Home in a Solo World

Marcus considered himself a Christian but avoided joining any church, preferring what he called "Jesus and me" faith. He attended services sporadically at different churches, never committing to any community. When his parents divorced and his faith wavered, he found himself isolated with no spiritual support system. It wasn't until he reluctantly joined a small group that he discovered what he'd been missing—people who knew his story, celebrated his victories, and walked with him through his struggles.

In a culture that prizes individual choice and personal spirituality, church membership can seem restrictive or unnecessary. Social media feeds us the illusion that we can build meaningful relationships through screens and maintain spiritual health through podcast sermons and inspirational quotes. But this approach ignores a fundamental truth about human nature and God's design for his people.

Biblical Christianity is inherently communal.

Just as you can't have a one-person family, you can't have a one-person church. The New Testament uses family language repeatedly when describing the church—brothers and sisters, adoption, inheritance, household of faith. This isn't accidental poetry; it's intentional theology. God designed us to grow spiritually within the context of committed relationships.

Membership isn't about institutional control or religious bureaucracy. It's about mutual commitment, shared responsibility, and spiritual family bonds that provide the foundation for authentic Christian growth. When we commit to a local church, we're saying we'll stick around long enough for real relationships to develop and for genuine transformation to happen.

Why membership matters:

- Mutual accountability helps believers grow in holiness and resist temptation through honest relationships
- Committed community provides stability during life's storms and spiritual dry seasons
- Shared mission becomes possible when people move beyond casual attendance to invested participation
- Spiritual authority operates properly when leaders know their flock and members trust their shepherds

Remember our discussion about becoming human again? This transformation happens best within the safety and challenge of committed community. When people know you well enough to call out your blind spots and love you enough to walk through your failures, real change becomes possible.

Elena initially resisted her youth pastor's encouragement to consider church membership, viewing it as "too serious" for a teenager. She enjoyed youth group but didn't want to be tied down to one church when she might move away for college. But when she watched her church rally around a family facing medical crisis—organizing meals, providing childcare, and covering expenses—she realized membership wasn't about rules but about becoming part of a family that shows up for each other.

She joined the church six months later, understanding that membership meant both receiving and giving this kind of committed love.

The solo Christian life seems attractive because it avoids the mess of dealing with difficult people, conflicting opinions, and organizational responsibilities. But it also misses the joy of shared celebration, the strength found in united prayer, and the growth that comes through serving others sacrificially.

Church membership teaches us that faith isn't a private hobby but a shared way of life. When we commit to a local congregation, we learn to love people we might not naturally choose as friends, to forgive quickly and completely, and to put others' needs before our own comfort.

This preparation matters more than we realize. As we'll explore in the next chapter, understanding our future hope changes how we live today, and much of that future involves eternal community with God's people. Learning to do community well now prepares us for the perfect community we'll experience then.

The church isn't perfect, but it's home.

Spotting Authentic Faith Communities

When Marcus moved to a new city for college, he visited dozens of churches trying to find the "perfect" one. Some had amazing music but shallow teaching. Others had solid doctrine but seemed cold and unwelcoming. Still others emphasized social justice but rarely mentioned sin or salvation. His campus minister helped him understand that while no church is perfect, there are biblical markers of healthy churches that should guide his decision.

Throughout history, Christians have identified key characteristics that distinguish authentic churches from religious organizations that may use Christian language but lack biblical substance. These marks aren't about worship style, building size, or denominational affiliation. They focus on the essential elements that make a gathering of people truly Christian rather than just religious.

These markers help believers evaluate not just which church to join, but how to contribute to their church's health and growth. Understanding these characteristics equips young Christians to make wise decisions about church involvement and to articulate what makes Christianity distinct from other religious movements.

The three historic marks of a true church:

- Faithful preaching and teaching of God's Word as the ultimate authority for faith and practice
- Proper administration of baptism and communion as Christ commanded
- Church discipline exercised with grace and truth to maintain holiness and unity

The first mark centers on Scripture's authority. A healthy church doesn't just read Bible verses or use Christian vocabulary—it submits to biblical truth even when that truth challenges popular culture or personal preferences. The preaching should regularly address sin, salvation, and sanctification, not just practical life tips or motivational speaking. When churches drift from biblical authority, they eventually lose their distinctive Christian character.

The second mark involves the sacraments or ordinances. Baptism should represent genuine conversion and public commitment to following Christ, not just family tradition or church membership ritual. Communion should be treated as sacred remembrance of Christ's sacrifice, celebrated with appropriate reverence and understanding. These practices connect us to two thousand years of Christian tradition and remind us of core gospel truths.

The third mark often makes people uncomfortable. Church discipline sounds harsh in our culture that avoids confrontation and prizes individual freedom. But biblical discipline isn't about punishment—it's about restoration. When church members fall into serious sin or teach false doctrine, loving correction protects both the individual and the congregation's witness.

Sarah felt confused when her friend invited her to a church that seemed more like a self-help seminar than worship. The messages focused on personal success and positive thinking, but rarely mentioned Jesus, sin, or salvation. The pastor quoted more from business books than the Bible, and communion was offered casually without any explanation of its meaning.

Using the marks of a true church as her guide, she recognized that while the people were friendly and the music was excellent, the absence of biblical preaching and gospel-centered teaching meant this wasn't a church that would help her grow in authentic faith. She kindly declined her friend's invitation while explaining what she was looking for in a church home.

Remember our journey through becoming human again? Authentic churches provide the environment where this transformation happens safely and effectively. They challenge us with God's truth while supporting us with God's grace.

These markers also connect to everything we've learned about God's character, Christ's work, and the Spirit's power. A church that neglects biblical authority can't properly represent the God who reveals himself through Scripture. A church that treats the sacraments carelessly diminishes the significance of what Christ accomplished. A church that avoids loving discipline fails to reflect God's holiness and mercy.

As we prepare to explore how future hope changes present living, remember that healthy churches point us toward that eternal reality while equipping us for faithful living today.

Sacred Rituals That Define Us

Marcus had been a Christian for two years but kept postponing baptism, partly from nervousness and partly because he didn't see why it mattered. "I'm already saved," he reasoned. But when his youth group studied the early church in Acts, he noticed that new believers were baptized immediately—not as an afterthought, but as an essential declaration of their new identity. At the next baptism service, watching candidates boldly proclaim their faith, he finally understood that baptism wasn't just a ritual but a public declaration of belonging to Christ and his church.

Baptism and communion (also called the Lord's Supper) serve as visible signs of invisible spiritual realities. These practices, commanded by Jesus himself, function like wedding rings in marriage —they don't create the relationship, but they publicly declare and regularly remind us of our commitment. For young believers navigating questions of identity and belonging, these ordinances provide concrete ways to express faith and connect with the global church across cultures and centuries.

Think of these practices as spiritual anchors. When emotions fluctuate and circumstances change, baptism and communion remind us of unchanging truths about who we are and whose we are.

Key meanings of the ordinances:

- Baptism represents dying to sin and rising to new life in Christ, marking the transition from old identity to new
- Communion regularly reminds believers of Christ's sacrifice and their unity with him and each other
- Both practices connect individual believers to the larger story of God's people throughout history

Baptism tells a complete story in one dramatic moment. Going under the water symbolizes burial with Christ—our old self dominated by sin dies and stays buried. Rising from the water represents resurrection to new life—we emerge as new creations with Christ's life flowing through us. This isn't just personal symbolism; it's a public declaration that we've switched sides in the cosmic battle between good and evil.

Communion operates differently but carries equal significance. Rather than a one-time declaration, it provides regular reminder and renewal. The bread represents Christ's body broken for us; the cup represents his blood shed for our forgiveness. Each time we participate, we're saying "yes" again to the gospel message and recommitting ourselves to following Christ.

Elena felt nervous about taking communion for the first time, worried she wasn't "good enough" or didn't understand it fully. Her small group leader explained that communion isn't for perfect people but for forgiven people—those who recognize their need for Christ's sacrifice. As she participated, she felt the weight of joining believers throughout history in remembering Jesus' death and anticipating his return. The simple act of bread and juice became a profound reminder of her identity as part of God's family, both locally and globally.

These ordinances also connect to everything we've learned throughout our journey. Remember the Trinity's ultimate plot twist? Communion celebrates the Son's sacrifice ordered by the Father and applied by the Spirit. Recall the great exchange nobody talks about? Baptism dramatizes our old life exchanged for Christ's righteousness. Think about the resurrection's game-changing power? Both ordinances point to the resurrection life we now possess.

The practices also prepare us for what's coming next. As we'll explore how future hope changes present living, remember that both baptism and communion are forward-looking. Baptism declares our participation in Christ's death and resurrection, anticipating our own bodily resurrection. Communion explicitly looks forward to the marriage supper of the Lamb when we'll feast with Christ in his kingdom.

These aren't empty religious rituals but powerful spiritual realities.

They anchor our identity in Christ's work rather than our performance, connect us to the global church family, and remind us that our story is part of God's much larger story of redemption and renewal.

You're right—let's strip those hyphens out and make it feel as natural as possible. Here is the revised, humanized **Theology Toolbox** for Chapter 11, focused on making the church feel like a home rather than an organization.

Chapter 11 Toolbox: The Family You Belong To

- **Visible and Invisible Church**: The visible church is the local group you can actually see and visit on a map. The invisible church is the much bigger spiritual family of every true believer across the world and throughout history.
- **Ordinances**: These are the two special rituals Jesus told us to keep doing: Baptism and Communion. They act like anchors that remind us who we belong to and what Jesus did for us.
- **Ecclesiology**: This is simply the study of why we need the church. It reminds us that God designed us to grow in a family of believers rather than trying to survive as a solo Christian.
- **Church Discipline**: This isn't about being mean or controlling people. It's actually a form of tough love where the church family helps someone get back on the right track when they start making choices that hurt themselves or others.

12

THE FUTURE THAT CHANGES
EVERYTHING TODAY

When Death Opens New Worlds

Death terrifies most people because it represents the ultimate unknown, the final goodbye, the end of everything we can touch and see. Yet Christianity presents one of its most shocking claims here: death, humanity's greatest enemy, has become the doorway to our greatest victory.

This sounds completely backwards until you understand what happened at the cross and empty tomb.

When sin entered the world through Adam and Eve's choice in the garden, death came with it like an unwelcome guest who never leaves. Death wasn't part of God's original design for humanity. We were created for life, relationship, and eternal connection with our Creator. But sin broke that connection, and death became the natural consequence of separation from the source of all life.

The Sting That Lost Its Power

Paul writes in 1 Corinthians that death once had a "sting" - a painful, poisonous bite that spelled doom for everyone. But Christ's resurrection changed everything. The sting has been removed. Death still happens, but it no longer has the final word.

Think of it like this: imagine a venomous snake that looks terrifying but has had its venom removed. It might still frighten you with its appearance, but it can't actually harm you anymore. Death looks the same as it always has, but for believers, its power to destroy has been completely broken.

Frederick watched his grandfather battle cancer with remarkable peace. While his non-Christian friends couldn't understand how his grandfather could joke and encourage others while dying, Frederick witnessed firsthand how belief in resurrection changes everything. His grandfather often said, "I'm not dying - I'm just changing addresses."

This perspective didn't eliminate grief. Frederick still cried when his grandfather passed away. But his sorrow was different from hopeless despair. It was the sadness of temporary separation, not permanent loss.

A Doorway, Not a Dead End

For believers, physical death becomes the gateway to spiritual life in its fullest form. This isn't just wishful thinking or denial about mortality. It's based on the historical reality of Christ's resurrection, which we explored in Chapter 8.

Because Jesus conquered death by dying and rising again, death can no longer hold believers captive. What once seemed like the ultimate defeat becomes the moment of ultimate victory. The body may fail, but the person - the soul, the essence of who they are - passes through death into eternal life with God.

Living Without Fear's Shadow

Understanding this truth transforms how Christians approach their own mortality and the death of loved ones. It doesn't make death pleasant or remove all sadness from loss. But it removes the sting of ultimate despair.

Daisy lost her best friend in a car accident during senior year. The grief was overwhelming, but her faith provided an anchor that her other friends didn't have. She knew this wasn't the end of their friendship - just a pause until they would meet again in God's presence.

This hope isn't escape from reality. It's engagement with a deeper reality than what we can see with our eyes.

Death's New Role

Death still exists, but its role has been completely rewritten in the Christian story. Instead of being the final chapter, it becomes a transition chapter. Instead of being the period at the end of life's sentence, it becomes the comma that leads to eternal life's beginning.

This understanding connects directly to everything we've learned about God's family in Chapter 11. Death cannot break the bonds that God creates between believers. Physical separation is temporary. The family relationships formed in Christ extend far beyond the grave into eternity itself.

Death has been transformed from humanity's greatest fear into Christianity's doorway to ultimate hope.

Between Heaven and Earth's Final Hour

The time between death and resurrection creates one of Christianity's most fascinating mysteries. What happens to believers who die before Christ returns? Where do they go? What are they doing? These questions have puzzled Christians for centuries, but Scripture provides some important clues about this in-between time.

When believers die, they don't simply cease to exist until the final resurrection. Paul writes in 2 Corinthians that to be absent from the body means being present with the Lord. This suggests that the moment of death marks an immediate transition into Christ's presence, not a long sleep or period of unconsciousness.

The Intermediate State

This period between individual death and the general resurrection is called the intermediate state. Believers experience conscious fellowship with Christ, but they haven't yet received their resurrected bodies.

Think of it like being in the most amazing waiting room ever created - you're exactly where you want to be, but you know something even better is coming.

This isn't the final destination. It's a wonderful pause before the ultimate reunion when Christ returns and all believers receive their resurrection bodies, just like Christ's body after Easter morning.

Uma struggled with anxiety about the future until she grasped the concept of Christ's return. She realized that her worry about college, career, and relationships stemmed from assuming she had to figure everything out herself. Understanding that history has a destination - Christ's return and the establishment of His kingdom - gave her a framework for making decisions.

She began asking, "How does this choice align with God's ultimate plan?" rather than "How can I control every outcome?"

The Second Coming's Certainty

Christ's second coming represents the culmination of everything we've explored throughout this book. The God who hides in plain sight will be revealed to everyone. The Bible's promises will find their complete fulfillment. The Trinity's rescue mission will reach its victorious conclusion.

Remember the resurrection's game-changing power from Chapter 8? Christ's return will extend that resurrection power to all believers who have died. Death's transformation from enemy to doorway will be complete when the last person passes through it into eternal life.

Living Between Two Worlds

We currently live in the "already but not yet" tension. Christ has already accomplished salvation through his death and resurrection. The Spirit already lives within believers, transforming them from the inside out. God's family already exists, providing love and support that transcends biological relationships.

But we're not yet experiencing the fullness of these realities.

We still struggle with sin's effects in our own hearts and in the world around us. Creation still groans under the weight of brokenness we explored in Chapter 5. Death still separates us from loved ones, even though its ultimate power has been broken.

Christ's return will resolve this tension completely. The "not yet" will become "now." The kingdom that exists partially will become the kingdom that exists fully.

Hope That Changes Today

This future certainty transforms present decisions. When you know the story's ending, you can navigate the middle chapters with confidence. When you understand that God's plan includes the complete restoration of everything broken by sin, you can work toward that restoration now.

Frank started volunteering at a homeless shelter after understanding Christ's return. He realized that caring for society's most vulnerable people wasn't just nice behavior - it was practice for the kind of world God is creating. His service became a way of bringing future hope into present reality.

Living With Expectant Hope

The intermediate state and second coming aren't just theological concepts for academic discussion. They're sources of daily hope and guidance. Knowing that death leads immediately to Christ's presence removes fear from mortality. Understanding that history has a definite destination provides purpose for today's choices.

This expectant hope connects everything we've learned about God's character, Christ's work, and the Spirit's transformation into a unified vision of ultimate hope.

When Heaven's Gavel Falls

The concept of final judgment makes many people uncomfortable, but it reveals something beautiful about God's character that we can't understand any other way. Without judgment, love becomes meaningless and justice becomes impossible. God's judgment isn't the angry outburst of a cosmic tyrant - it's the careful verdict of a perfect judge who cares deeply about right and wrong.

Marcus used to think that a loving God couldn't judge anyone. But when his sister was sexually assaulted, his perspective shifted dramatically. He realized that a God who didn't judge evil wasn't loving at all - He would be indifferent to victims and injustice. The doctrine of final judgment became a source of comfort, knowing that even if earthly courts failed, perfect justice would ultimately prevail.

At the same time, understanding God's mercy helped him forgive his sister's attacker, knowing that even the worst sinners could find redemption through Christ.

Justice That Actually Matters

Every day we witness terrible injustices that never get resolved. Corrupt politicians escape consequences. Bullies never face accountability. Victims never see their attackers punished. This creates a deep sense that the universe is fundamentally unfair - that good and evil don't really matter in the end.

God's final judgment addresses this problem directly. Every act of cruelty, every moment of selfishness, every choice to harm instead of help - none of it will be ignored or forgotten. Perfect justice will finally be served, not because God enjoys punishment, but because He loves victims too much to let evil go unpunished.

This doesn't mean God is waiting to catch us doing wrong like some cosmic police officer. It means that moral choices actually have weight and meaning beyond what we can see in this life.

Mercy That Transforms Everything

But here's where Christianity's understanding of judgment becomes revolutionary. God doesn't just provide perfect justice - He also provides perfect mercy through Christ's work that we explored in Chapters 6 and 7.

The same God who will judge every wrong action also became human and took that judgment upon himself at the cross. This isn't God changing the rules or overlooking sin. This is God satisfying justice while providing mercy at incredible personal cost.

Remember the great exchange from Chapter 7? Christ took our guilt so we could receive His righteousness. This means that believers face judgment, but they face it with Christ's perfect record instead of their own flawed one.

Two Destinations, One Choice

Scripture describes two eternal destinations: heaven and hell. These aren't arbitrary assignments based on God's mood. They're the natural outcomes of our fundamental choice about God himself.

Heaven represents eternal life in perfect relationship with God, surrounded by the family we discussed in Chapter 11. It's the restoration of everything that was broken in the fall from Chapter 5, magnified into perfect and permanent joy.

Hell represents eternal separation from God - the source of all love, joy, peace, and hope. It's not primarily about fire and torture, though those images communicate real suffering. It's about the ultimate loneliness of being cut off from the source of all good things.

Judgment That Validates Our Choices

God's judgment vindicates the importance of the decisions we make every day. When we choose to follow Christ, when we treat others with kindness, when we stand up against injustice - these choices matter eternally.

Sarah struggled with depression because she felt like nothing she did made any difference in the world. Learning about final judgment helped her understand that her small acts of love and service had eternal significance. God notices and remembers every cup of cold water given in His name.

Living Under Perfect Justice and Perfect Mercy

Understanding final judgment should create both healthy fear and incredible hope. Fear that motivates us to take our relationship with

God seriously. Hope that assures us perfect justice will ultimately triumph and perfect mercy is available right now.

This judgment isn't something distant and theoretical. It's the climax toward which all of history is moving - the moment when heaven's gavel falls and everything becomes clear.

Paradise Reimagined Beyond Golden Stereotypes

Most people imagine eternity as an endless church service where everyone floats around on clouds playing harps. This stereotypical view of heaven has caused countless people to wonder if eternal life would actually be boring rather than wonderful. But the biblical picture of eternity looks nothing like these golden stereotypes - it's far more exciting and meaningful than most Christians realize.

Chelsea always pictured heaven as boring - floating on clouds playing harps forever. This misconception made her question whether she even wanted eternal life. But studying Revelation 21-22 revolutionized her understanding. She discovered that eternity involves a renewed earth with cities, nations, culture, and meaningful work. As someone passionate about environmental science, she realized that her calling to care for creation aligned with God's ultimate plan to renew all things.

This gave her studies eternal significance and made her excited about the future rather than dreading endless boredom.

A New Earth, Not Escape From Earth

The Bible's vision of eternity centers on "new heavens and a new earth" rather than a purely spiritual existence somewhere far away. This represents the complete renewal of physical reality, not its abandonment. God doesn't plan to destroy creation and start over - He plans to transform and perfect the creation He originally called "very good" in Chapter 4.

Remember how sin corrupted creation in Chapter 5, subjecting it to decay and death? The new earth reverses all of that corruption completely. Every beautiful aspect of our current world - mountains, oceans, forests, animals - will exist in perfected form without any trace of sin's damage.

Resurrection Bodies for Physical Reality

Our resurrection bodies, which we discussed earlier in this chapter, make perfect sense when you understand that eternity involves physical reality. Just as Christ's resurrection body was recognizably physical but gloriously transformed, our new bodies will be perfectly suited for life on the new earth.

These bodies won't be subject to disease, aging, or death. They'll be capable of experiences and activities we can barely imagine. Think about how much joy you can experience in your current body despite its limitations - then multiply that by infinity for a body designed for perfect eternal existence.

Culture, Work, and Creativity Redeemed

The new earth won't be a place where everyone does identical activities for eternity. Revelation describes nations bringing their glory and honor into the New Jerusalem, suggesting that human culture, diversity, and creativity will find their ultimate expression in eternity.

This means that current pursuits in art, science, technology, music, literature, and countless other fields aren't just temporary diversions - they're previews of the kind of meaningful work and creative expression that will continue forever in perfected form.

David struggled to see how his passion for music connected to his faith until he understood this vision of eternity. Realizing that his musical gifts would find their ultimate fulfillment in the new creation gave him motivation to develop his talents as an act of worship and preparation for eternal service.

No More Separation Between Sacred and Secular

In the new earth, there will be no distinction between sacred and secular activities because God's presence will fill everything completely. Work won't be toilsome drudgery but joyful participation in God's ongoing creative activity. Relationships won't be complicated by sin but will express perfect love in countless creative ways.

The family bonds we explored in Chapter 11 will reach their ultimate expression when the entire redeemed community lives together in perfect harmony with God and each other.

Living Now With Eternal Perspective

Understanding the true nature of eternity transforms how we view current activities and responsibilities. Caring for the environment isn't just practical stewardship - it's practice for the renewed earth. Developing skills and talents isn't just personal fulfillment - it's preparation for eternal service. Building relationships isn't just emotional satisfaction - it's investing in bonds that will last forever.

This vision replaces the boring stereotype of eternity with an exciting picture of adventure, creativity, relationships, and meaningful work that never ends but only gets better.

Chapter 12 Toolbox: The Best is Yet to Come

- **Intermediate State:** This is the "holding pattern" for believers who die before Jesus returns; they go immediately to be with Him while they wait for the final resurrection .
- **Eschatology:** This is the study of "the end," which isn't about being afraid of the future, but about understanding that God has a specific destination for history.
- **Final Judgment:** This is the moment when "heaven's gavel falls" and God finally makes every wrong thing right and brings perfect justice to the world .
- **The New Earth:** This is the ultimate "happily ever after"—a physical world that has been perfectly restored where we will live, work, and create with God forever .

AFTERWORD

Throughout this journey into systematic theology, we've been building something extraordinary together—an unshakeable faith foundation that can withstand the real-world challenges you'll face in college, career, and beyond. This isn't just academic knowledge stored away for future reference; it's a living framework that transforms how you understand yourself, your relationships, and your purpose in the world.

Systematic theology serves as your intellectual and spiritual GPS, helping you navigate life's biggest questions with confidence and clarity. When your professor challenges the reliability of Scripture, when friends question why a good God allows suffering, or when you wrestle with doubts about your own beliefs, you now have more than just feelings or traditions to fall back on—you have a coherent, biblically-grounded understanding of who God is and how He works in the world.

The vision we've pursued isn't about turning you into a professional theologian, but about equipping you to live as a thoughtful, confident believer who can engage meaningfully with both supporters and skeptics. You're now prepared to discuss complex theological concepts in ways that are accessible and relevant, connecting eternal truths to the daily decisions and relationships that shape your life.

Key Truths We've Discovered

God reveals himself progressively through creation and Scripture. We began by understanding that theology isn't human speculation about the divine, but God's own self-revelation. Through general revelation in creation and special revelation in Scripture, God has made himself knowable. This means your faith isn't built on wishful thinking but on God's intentional communication with humanity.

The Trinity shows us that relationship is fundamental to reality. Perhaps no doctrine seemed more abstract at first, yet the Trinity proves to be profoundly practical. Understanding God as Father, Son, and Holy Spirit—three persons in perfect unity—reveals that relationship isn't just something God does, it's who God is. This transforms how you approach your own relationships, showing you that community, love, and unity aren't optional extras but reflections of God's very nature.

Jesus' incarnation, death, and resurrection accomplish comprehensive salvation. The person and work of Christ stand at the center of everything. Jesus isn't just a great teacher or moral example—He's the God-man who accomplished what no one else could. His incarnation bridges the gap between divine and human, His death satisfies God's justice while expressing His love, and His resurrection guarantees your future hope while empowering your present transformation.

The Spirit empowers transformation and mission. The Holy Spirit isn't just a mysterious force but a personal presence who applies Christ's work to your life. Through the Spirit, you experience regeneration, sanctification, and empowerment for ministry. This means the Christian life isn't about trying harder but about yielding to the Spirit's transforming power.

The church provides community and accountability. Ecclesiology reveals that faith isn't meant to be private or individualistic. The church serves as God's chosen method for spiritual growth, mutual encouragement, and corporate witness. Your local church becomes the place where theological truths get lived out in real relationships with real people facing real challenges.

Future hope shapes present living. Eschatology isn't just about satisfying curiosity about the future—it's about understanding how God's ultimate plan gives meaning and direction to your current choices.

What This Means for Your Life

- Theology is practical—it shapes how you live, love, and make decisions
- Questions and doubts are part of mature faith, not threats to it
- Your faith can withstand intellectual scrutiny and real-world testing
- You're part of a story bigger than yourself that gives ultimate meaning to your choices

Your Next Steps

Continue studying Scripture with what you have learned in mind. Do not treat theology as something you finish and move on from. Bring these ideas into your personal Bible reading and your group conversations. When you read Scripture, pay attention to how the truths connect and build on one another. Let theology help you see the bigger picture of what God is doing, not just isolated verses.

Look for a local church where you can live out these truths with other people. Faith was never meant to be lived alone. Learning about God without sharing life with other believers leaves something unfinished. Find a church where you can worship, serve, ask questions, and grow alongside others. Do more than sit and listen. Step in. Participate. Let what you know shape how you love and serve the people around you.

You will also encounter people who disagree with what you believe. That is normal. Your theological foundation is not meant to win arguments, but it does give you confidence to speak clearly and listen carefully. As you talk with classmates, coworkers, and neighbors who see the world differently, practice explaining your beliefs with humility and respect. Pay attention to their stories. Look for ways your faith can be shown through patience, kindness, and grace, not just words.

Finally, develop habits that deepen your relationship with God. Let what you know about God shape how you pray and worship. Let your understanding of spiritual growth push you toward a life that reflects what you believe. Practices like prayer, service, and self discipline are not about earning God's approval. They are ways of staying connected to Him as you grow.

The goal is not just to know more about God.

The goal is to walk with Him.

Living It Out

Finn is a friend of mine who moved to another town a few years ago. Not long ago, he wrote to me about how this book and others like it had shaped the way he thought during a difficult season in his life.

When his parents divorced during his sophomore year of high school, everything felt unstable. But instead of losing his faith or growing bitter, Finn found himself returning to the truths we had talked about together. He leaned on what he understood about God's sovereignty, the reality of sin, and the hope of redemption.

Those ideas did not remove the pain, but they gave him a way to face it honestly. His theological foundation helped him respond with grace rather than resentment and allowed him to hold on to hope, even when healing felt slow and uncertain.

Similarly, Uma shared how her understanding of the Trinity revolutionized her approach to relationships. She began to see her friendships and family connections through the lens of God's relational nature. Her theological foundation gave her wisdom for setting healthy boundaries, extending grace during conflicts, and pursuing unity without compromising truth.

These stories remind us that theology matters not because it makes us smarter but because it makes us wiser.

As you move forward, carry these truths with confidence. When you face intellectual challenges to your faith, remember that Christianity has weathered every storm and emerged stronger. When you encounter suffering that seems to contradict God's goodness, recall that the cross demonstrates God's willingness to enter into our pain and transform it for His glory. When you're tempted to live for temporary pleasures or achievements, let your eschatological hope, your belief about the future of the Kingdom of God. Remind you that you're citizens of a kingdom that cannot be shaken.

The theological foundation you've built will serve you well in your daily life and wherever it leads you, including the graduation stage, college lecture halls, corporate boardrooms, and hospital waiting rooms. You're equipped now to think Christianly about every aspect of human experience, to love deeply because you understand how deeply you've been loved, and to hope confidently because you know how the story ends.

May you live with the joy that comes from knowing your Creator, the peace that flows from understanding your salvation, and the purpose that emerges from grasping your calling.

Go forward with confidence!

Conclusion Toolbox: Your Life Map

- **Orthodoxy and Orthopraxy:** This is a simple way of saying that what you believe (*orthodoxy*) should always change the way you actually live your life (*orthopraxy*).
- **Living the Story:** This is the shift from just reading about God to actually walking with Him, letting theology be the "GPS" for every decision you make

www.ingramcontent.com/pod-product-compliance
Lightning Source LLC
Chambersburg PA
CBHW061650120626
46550CB00003B/895

* 9 7 8 1 9 5 7 5 1 5 5 1 9 *